LITERACY

LITERACY

Teaching and Learning Language Skills

Edited by
ASHER CASHDAN

Basil Blackwell

© Basil Blackwell Ltd 1986

First published 1986

Basil Blackwell Ltd
108 Cowley Road, Oxford OX4 1JF, UK

Basil Blackwell Inc.
432 Park Avenue South, Suite 1505,
New York, NY 10016, USA

British Library Cataloguing in Publication Data

Literacy : teaching and learning language skills.
  1. Language arts
  I. Cashdan, Asher
  401'.9   LB1575.8
    ISBN 0–631–13554–5
    ISBN 0–631–14279–7 Pbk

Library of Congress Cataloging in Publication Data
Main entry under title:

Literacy : teaching and learning language skills.

  Includes index.
  Contents: Language and the curriculum/Asher Cashdan – Styles of interaction and opportunities for learning/Gordon Wells – Cognitive processes in reading and spelling/Geoffrey and Jean Underwood – [etc.]
  1. Language arts–Addresses, essays, lectures. 2. Reading–Addresses, essays, lectures. 3. Learning–Addresses, essays, lectures. 4. Literacy–Addresses, essays, lectures. I. Cashdan, Asher.
LB1576.L56   1986   372.6   85–18705
ISBN 0–631–13554–5
ISBN 0–631–14279–7 (pbk.)

Typeset by Oxford Publishing Services, Oxford
Printed in Great Britain by Bell and Bain Ltd., Glasgow

Contents

vi

Introduction

In an industrial society, the needs for literacy are obvious, whether at work or in private life. So it is not surprising that schools have always paid considerable attention to this side of their teaching. Furthermore, the advent of the new technologies is likely to make greater rather than fewer demands on literacy skills. As David Williams explains later in this book, working with computers enforces the necessity to be particularly precise in both analysing written output and planning one's own input.

There is another important point here. Literacy is not simply a matter of decoding print to sounds, or of converting sounds to print. It involves meaning. All of us – children and adults alike – are constantly occupied in making meanings. It is not enough for us to comprehend a text to the extent of being able to repeat it, or even to explain what it says 'in our own words', although this is a beginning. Full comprehension means understanding what the writer (or speaker) means by reference to what has not been said as well as what has, by comparison with material, ideas and knowledge outside the immediate text and by analysis of the writer's purposes and of how the message has been coded – its language, style, register or code.

In other words, full literacy involves the use of many inputs over and above the immediate message, in terms both of content and of analysis. Analysis, however, cannot be practised in a vacuum. If the message is empty, saying nothing and being part of no context – cognitive or affective – for the recipient, then no analysis is possible. Philosophers used to offer the sentence 'the army is on night manoeuvres' to make the point about context. Said in a barrack-room in a particular place on a particular date, the sentence means a great deal. Read on this page today with no elaboration, we can do nothing beyond offering definitions of the words in the sentence and a few speculations about how it could *become* meaningful.

In the aftermath of the Bullock report (DES (Department of Education and Science), 1975) I persuaded some colleagues to provide the material for a reader on language, reading and learning (Cashdan, 1979). Along with chapters on linguistic approaches, assessment, primary and secondary methodology, etc., we included two specifically on literature, both for their own sake and to make the point that reading would be a barren, sterile activity unless we paid due attention to the content of what was read. In the current book, we hope to have gone further and to have integrated form and content to the point where a chapter on either separately would make no sense. Not only that, we feel that chapters on language as an entity, or on reading on its own, make little sense either. Both John Merritt and I argue specifically later in this book that reading and language have no inherent value except as tools for learning. It may be a measure of the success of the 'language across the curriculum' movement that educationists now consider reading and language as valuable in their own right. But this is a misunderstanding – and it is a major purpose of this book to demonstrate how important it still is, ten years after the Bullock report, to pursue literacy energetically, but a total concept of creating and making meanings.

The book opens with two background chapters. First a survey of language in the curriculum which I hope will set the stage for considering literacy as an integral part of the whole of school (and later) learning. This is followed by Gordon Wells' analysis, based on his major research project at Bristol, of determinants of meaning-making in young children and their implications for teachers. After these come three chapters which provide detailed analyses of current research and thinking in literacy study: the Underwoods on cognitive processes, Colin Harrison on newer thinking on readability and John Harris on the fast-growing study of children's writing and its development. The succeeding three chapters cover selected growth points at a more consciously applied level. Helen Arnold emphasises the emptiness of much hearing of reading and offers positive help; David Wray does a parallel job with project work; and David Williams demonstrates entertainingly the range of pedagogical possibilities opened up (but as yet largely unexploited) by the classroom computer. Peter Brinton then looks at assessment, particularly as it normally happens, in the classroom. Finally, John Merritt offers some salutary thoughts on the danger we are still open to, of inert thinking. To be blunt, as indeed he is, chapters such as those by the Underwoods and Harrison in this book would, following Merritt's analysis, be of no use in either teaching or teacher-training unless read with full engagement, including a constant and active searching for meanings and applications. Full literacy entails very hard work!

Asher Cashdan

References

Cashdan, A. (ed.) (1979) *Language, Reading and Learning*. Basil Blackwell.
DES (1975) *A Language for Life* (The Bullock report). HMSO.

1

Language and the curriculum

Asher Cashdan

Introduction

It must now be something like twenty years since groups of teachers, particularly those involved in English teaching, began to study what came to be called 'language across the curriculum'. They focused attention, not just on the language of the pupil, but on that of the teacher also. Their concerns reached a wide public, both through the work of the National Association for the Teaching of English (NATE) and, perhaps even more, through the publication of two seminal books. The more applied of these texts was undoubtedly 'Language, the Learner and the School' (Barnes, Britton and Rosen, 1969) and the more theoretical, 'Language and Learning' (Britton, 1970). In 1971, NATE devoted a whole issue of 'English in Education' to this subject. Its editors (Clements and Griffiths, 1971) summarised the main issues as follows. They asked teachers:

> to pause a while to consider the language they use to teach with and the language they ask pupils to learn with. We need to understand more about how we can help our pupils to use language, both spoken and written, to make sense of their own lives and what they learn in school. We need to listen more carefully to what our pupils say. We need to structure our work with them in such a way that they use language as productively as possible.

They go on to emphasise that language for learning is thus of significance for all teachers, not only for English teachers.

This is a clear enough statement, yet it is not surprising that it has been interpreted in a wide variety of ways. And although the influence of the 'language' movement is undeniable, its success has been variable. It is the purpose of this chapter to look at some of the issues involved in examining language in the curriculum, to evaluate current practice and to make a few tentative suggestions.

Philosophies of learning

All teachers make use of a philosophy (or psychology) of learning. That is only to say that, in teaching someone else, we make assumptions about the other person's capacities, learning techniques and, often enough, about their interests and attitudes. Even among trained teachers this philosophy, or learning theory, is largely unconscious, implicit and unthought-out. This intuitiveness of approach, which I would argue applies particularly in secondary teaching, may be due in part to the incompleteness, or unsatisfactory nature, of the psychology of learning, particularly as it is taught in the colleges of education. Thus, some differences between teachers' approaches may be attributable to the espousal of different textbook theories, e.g. more commitment to Piagetian, cognitive or stimulus-response psychologies. But even where teachers pay lip-service to a particular theoretical approach, it is often far from certain that their teaching, as they carry it out in practice, relates at all closely to the claimed theoretical stance. Thus (fortunately, some might say) those who claim to use behaviour modification techniques rarely demonstrate in practice the consistency that one would expect from them. And claims that 'in my classroom there is a great deal of pupil talk' are regularly belied by observational studies!

In practice, then, variation in approach to teaching probably owes more to teachers' personality and social background, to their attitudes to children and to their general political stance, than to their formal training. No doubt, of course, these background factors are passed through the filters of experience, study and training; nevertheless, it is the background factors that matter most; though, before passing on, it is probably worth stressing how great may be the influence of the ethos of the school or the department in which the teacher is working.

One might crudely categorise teachers' approaches into two broad groupings. Group A believe (or operate as if they did) that pupils learn by listening to teacher-talk; inattention/ failure is due to laziness or wickedness. It may also be due to the teacher talk being poorly executed – the teacher may be under-prepared, or may not have explained clearly. As a last resort (the first for some!), the pupil may lack the inherent ability for studying the subject or may come from a home which has not prepared him or her adequately for the school experience. Group B operate with a quite different set of assumptions. They believe that pupils learn by making their own contributions (including their own mistakes), through group work, self-directed learning and so on.

We could throw in a number of other modifiers – within each of our notional groups there may be quite a range of belief in/acceptance of individual and group differences. This could lead, even with Group A teachers, to the planning of group work, to modification of teaching materials as well as, as it more frequently does, to the creation of schemes for 'homogenising' the classroom: the well-known apparatus of streaming, setting, banding. Similarly, A teachers will tend to run authoritarian classrooms where teachers make the major decisions and B teachers may be so democratic that (as Bennett, 1978, claims) their children may spend more time deciding how to organise their learning than in actually learning anything. However that may be, B teachers will certainly tend to stress small group work and pupils learning from each other, perhaps begging the question (in A teachers' opinions) of how far they can in fact do so.

Teaching in practice

The above characterisation may be more than a little crude. There can, however, be no doubt that many pedagogic practices flow from our teachers' theoretical positions. Let us consider a few of these; they need not be taken as neat and tidy dichotomies, but as teachers belong more or less to our groups A or B, one can easily work out which of them they will tend to use more, less, or not at all.

1 The pupils work heavily from text books, write unseen examinations, and spend a lot of their time learning off 'facts'.
2 Pupils make heavy use of individualised work cards, of learning laboratories, of 'packs'.
3 There is much project work, paying conscious attention to information accessing skills and to the evaluation of writers' ideas and opinions.
4 Pupils are experienced in working together in groups, in collective projects, in discussion.
5 Much work is produced in formal, 'final draft' form, is impersonal and makes heavy use of the passive voice.
6 Pupils' work is frequently encouraged to be tentative, exploratory and unpolished and often makes use of new media (tapes, video).
7 Pupils are assessed by formal means and by coursework rather than end-of-course examinations.

The advocates of a 'language across the curriculum' approach, led by Barnes, Britton and Rosen (in their 1969 book) argued forcefully against too much final draft work and for a sensitivity to audience. This latter brought in its train an awareness of types of writing – Britton's categories of transactional, expressive and poetic. Of course, these categories have come under attack (and Beard (1984) makes a good case for replacing them with Kinneavy's model of Writer, Audience, Text and The World); but their enduring value is in this drawing the attention of pupil – and teacher – to the need for different styles in different contexts and for different purposes. (See Harris's chapter in this book for a more detailed discussion of approaches to drafting and of writing types.)

Language development

Through the whole range of philosophy and of practice outlined above, there runs nevertheless a commitment, shared by virtually all teachers, to the expectation that pupils will do most of their learning through language (an expectation, incidentally, not entirely shared by Piaget). Similarly, there is the assumption that a significant part of the teacher's task is to develop the pupils' language. Here, however, there is a considerable divergence of view. According to some theories, the pupil's language simply develops by exposure – exposure that is, to the teacher, the textbook and to the educational process in general. Practice is thought to help, though it may be divorced from the context in which it would be relevant; but, above all, the pupil progresses with maturation, so that deliberate planning is hardly needed. In the other camp, language development is seen to need very definite 'fostering' techniques. Similar differences occur in respect of the need to teach study skills to help children to learn how to read for different purposes, extract information, make notes, observe and record. For the moment, let us leave aside the question of whether 'language development' is an achievable, or even a desirable goal. We shall return to this question later.

Teachers' behaviour

As already implied, there is considerable variation in our self-awareness as teachers. In fact, most of us are distinctly lacking in self-knowledge. By this I mean nothing very subtle: most of us are unaware of how much we talk, whether we favour boys or girls, or which type of pupils we talk to more, whether by race, social background, personality or our evaluations of their potential abilities. This shows particularly in intervention studies, whether in the nursery or the secondary school. Teachers often claim that they do their teaching 'in context'; that is to say, they teach their pupils thinking skills, or English style, or whatever, by working on these skills during an on-going activity. Yet in many hours of observation, Wood, McMahon and Cranstoun (1980) found very little of this kind of 'on the job' activity, an experience very similar to that of an American team of researchers quoted in the Bullock report (DES, 1975). Another aspect of this lack of self-awareness is our surprise when we hear what children actually do in school. For instance, Lunzer and his team (Lunzer and Gardner, 1979) discovered how rare it is in secondary school for children to read continuously for longer than three minutes at a stretch (half of classroom reading occurring in 'bursts of less than fifteen seconds'), and Torbe (1980) found much the same in the secondary schools which he studied less formally.

Furthermore, teachers often think that their behaviour is responsive to pupil requests or needs. Yet Wood, McMahon and Cranstoun (1980) again showed that 'adults who managed a good deal were also approached for management, while those who interacted with children in talk, play and making things were approached more often for personal interactions.' Moreover they argue convincingly from their data that the pupils were responding to the teacher, not vice versa. As they put it, 'management seemed to breed more management, interactions more interactions.' (See Wells' chapter in this book where he quotes his own and Tizard's findings on conversation in nursery and infant classrooms.)

Part of the reason for this mismatch between what happens and what we think happens, lies in the undoubted difficulty of monitoring our own behaviour while busy at work. But there is little doubt that part also is due to a kind of

wish-fulfilment syndrome – we come to believe that those
things go on that we would like to be seeing, however
infrequently they actually happen in practice! And even when
we are engaged in interaction with pupils, it takes considerable self-monitoring for us to realise how frequently our
interactions lack sophistication and appropriateness. So often
our questions are closed and simple when they could be open
and exploratory, leading to pupil-initiated sequences, rather
than being 'stage-managed' by the teacher. (Another perspective on this problem is provided in Arnold's discussion of
hearing reading in her chapter in this book.)

Teachers' expectations

What do teachers assume (or demand) of their pupils' spoken
and written language? Some of their expectations could be set
out as follows.

1 Pupils ought to speak in standard English, using received
   pronunciation (BBC English, middle class London etc.).
2 Pupils should speak in well-formed sentences.
3 Pupils should write in standard English, using only
   well-formed sentences.
4 Pupils should use a variety of styles, tailoring these to the
   demands of the task and context. (Although Britton's
   categories of transactional, expressive and poetic are no
   longer as fashionable as they were, many would still wish
   to distinguish between functional and more personal
   writing).
5 Teachers should accept their pupils' home language,
   dialect, code/register. Alternatively, they should work
   from these, slowly weaning their pupils from them
   towards 'standard' expressions. Some would even suggest a complete break from the home language and the
   establishing from the start of a norm for school language.
   In contrast to these attitudes would be the evaluation of

the home dialect as equally effective and appropriate as standard English, or again the view that only standard English has the capacity to sustain subtle, abstract, disembedded thought, such as is needed in the educational system.

Subject demands

A particular concern of those interested in language across the curriculum has been the examination of the demands made in different school subjects. There is the question of readability. Not only are many school texts inadequately tailored to the reading abilities of the pupils (as when pupils are asked to work from material which is far too difficult, whether in literary style, scientific vocabulary or complexity of concepts); the same problem may apply also to the language of the home-made work-card or to the teacher's own speech. Furthermore, many secondary school subjects have their own particular vocabularies and modes of thought; it is a major aspect of the pupils' learning to get inside the language of the subject and its procedures. Yet this is often expected with no specific training and little insight into why literary work may demand one style and physics another.

Finally, as Crystal (1979) has demonstrated clearly, the decision as to what to correct and what to leave alone in pupils' writing at any particular stage needs to be based on accurate assessment of where that pupil has reached – in other words the judgement must be based on the pupil's 'grammar', not by reference to the final goals of adult style. Not only that, but there is a world of difference, as he points out, between exercises on 'sentence-connecting adverbials' and word games which may have the same object (Charlip's 'fortunately . . . unfortunately . . .'). Yet there is a persistent confusion among educators over what explicit language 'knowledge' pupils should have. Thus HMI (Her Majesty's Inspectorate: DES, 1984) have recently listed ten categories of language knowledge they expect of 11 year olds, including parts of speech, subject and object etc.

The relevance of educational aims

All of the above considerations need to be moderated in terms of what the teacher considers to be the object of both the particular and the general exercise. The kinds of questions that arise here include whether learning is an activity which is of value now, or whether one is always preparing only for distant goals. In the preceding section, for instance, one must distinguish between the needs of the budding physicist and those of the pupil whose interest in physical concepts is genuine enough but who is unlikely to devote the next two years (let alone the whole of his or her working life) to activity in this field. Again, one has to ask whether school is essentially a conservative agency, in which case the teacher's main purpose is to transmit existing standards and values, or whether it may be an agent for change. If the latter, then newer approaches to the nature of knowledge, its permanence and the context in which it is acquired, may become much more relevant. And if school cannot be a change agent, does this mean for many of us that we have again to consider de-schooling society?

'Language across the curriculum' today

What I have been trying to suggest throughout this chapter is that there are a number of ways in which language and its place in the curriculum can be approached. Teachers will differ in the emphasis they put upon different aspects and there are many areas in which they will not always agree with each other. For some, 'language across the curriculum' certainly means radical changes in the way in which the pupil is helped to approach the curriculum, involving changes in relationships and a more child-centred curriculum than hitherto, extending right through the secondary school. Others will see it more narrowly in terms of an agreed policy about correcting pupils' work, an examination of the vocabularies of different subjects, or even a greater sophistication about what teachers actually do, including detailed analysis of questioning techniques, criterion referenced approaches in assessment, or again perhaps a broader approach to comprehension, looking outside the text as well as inside it.

Supposing, however, we take 'language across the curriculum' as defined by the NATE editorial; how far have we progressed in the last ten years or so? Certainly there have been innovative schools, concerned local authorities, plenty of good writing, interesting courses and conferences. There are the books by Barnes (1973, 1976); the NATE Guidelines (1976), collections by Marland (1977) and Cashdan (1979) among many others. More recently, there is the report of the Talk Workshop Group (1982), in which staff of a school explore their work with pupils in considerable and fascinating detail. And interest has spread into further education, too (see Moor, 1985).

With all this, however, there is somehow the feeling that educationalists are pushing the same doctrines as in the sixties, rather than developing further. And the rash of so-called 'language' books with which we are covered fool few of us – so many are the old English exercises dressed up in new clothes.

Recent visits to Scotland have made me read carefully the very short, but highly significant, progress report of their HMIs on the education of pupils with learning difficulties (SED (Scottish Education Department), 1978). What did they find there but the same old phonic drills, the detachment of slower learners from their fellows, decreased motivation and irrelevant educational experience. Their recipes for improvement are on the right lines – they see the problem as in the curriculum (and school organisation) rather than in the pupil. Here again is enough evidence that there is still a long way to go (and even this report slips into advocating 'language for its own sake').

Some concluding principles

What, then, is there to do? We can of course keep spreading the established facts – writing, holding conferences, providing inservice courses. Such activities are not to be despised – and we can certainly point to some successes and some growth points. There is a movement to examine much more carefully than has been done so far the whole question of the language of different subjects and its implications in the secondary school. (See, for example, Gillham, 1985.) Innovations in the system, whether 'language' posts, school-based courses, Open University initiatives or other inservice work, may all help (and see Merritt's chapter). Also validating bodies such as CNAA (Council for National Academic Awards) do seem to be taking seriously the need for all pre-service courses to pay serious attention to language in the classroom. All of these will help, especially where a Local Education Authority, its advisers and its head teachers all pull together, so that language is not just a preoccupation of a tired, junior and badly-supported English teacher!

Have we anything more than this to offer? There are the beginnings of greater sophistication in the pragmatics of language, with some linguistics experts starting to approach the important questions in a more meaningful and applied way. I would cite the work of David Crystal, as mentioned above, and that of Katharine Perera (1984). Meanwhile, there are three principles which may well be worth pondering.

1 Much more effort needs to be put into heightening our self-awareness. Teachers do not know how much they talk in the classroom, what kinds of questions they employ, how their interaction style may be perceived by children – not because they are hypocritical, but because of the tremendous difficulty, in the 'heat of action', of monitoring their own

behaviour. We need to spend more time observing in each other's classrooms, using tape-recorders, above all in analysing our own performance. This may be thought of in terms of the new 'accountability' vogue, but it is accountability to ourselves that matters rather than the external imposition of the paymaster!

2 We need to spend much more thought on the reconciliation of direct and indirect approaches in teaching. Direct teaching is not to be dismissed. Curiously, the Bullock report (DES, 1975) in one and the same paragraph says 'explicit instruction out of context is in our view of little value' and then immediately talks of the need to keep a check-list, and to cover punctuation, some aspects of usage, the way words are built and the company they keep, and a knowledge of the modest collection of technical terms useful for the discussion of language! Provided that pupils and teachers share a common understanding of what needs to be done and why and, as Bullock again put it, that the need 'creates the opportunity', we really can hope to marry direct and opportunistic work. But this needs very careful working out, for what is being here advocated is the encapsulation of all true teaching – and it is too easy to get the balance wrong as I have suggested has happened in the recent HMI pamphlet (DES, 1984).

3 Above all, we must avoid the teaching of language for its own sake – and this includes 'language development'. We do need to learn to transfer, to acquire skills in one context that will generalise to many others; but language should always be a tool and not a master. It is ours for the solving of problems, for the achievement of goals (whether instructional, aesthetic or more purely recreational), but it has little justification as an abstract possession in its own right.

As Douglas Barnes himself says (Barnes, undated), 'In a way what we're doing has very little to do with language . . . We're trying to persuade teachers to adopt a reflective attitude to the teaching and learning that goes on in their lessons, and insofar as this is looking at language, then it's language.'

Asher Cashdan

Note

An earlier version of this chapter was published in *Reading through the Curriculum*, edited by Bruce Gillham (United Kingdom Reading Association/Heinemann, 1983).

References

Barnes, D. (1973) *Language in the Classroom* (E262, Block 4). Open University Press.
Barnes, D. (1976) *From Communication to Curriculum*. Penguin.
Barnes, D. (undated, circa 1980) *Language Across the Curriculum*. NATE (Coventry) Lecture Notes, No. 1.
Barnes, D., Britton, J. and Rosen, H. (1969) *Language, the Learner and the School*. Penguin.
Beard, R. (1984) *Children's Writing in the Primary School*. Hodder/UKRA.
Bennett, S.N. (1978) 'Recent research on teaching', *British Journal of Educational Psychology*, 48, 127-47.
Britton, J. (1970) *Language and Learning*. Penguin.
Cashdan, A. (ed.) (1979) *Language, Reading and Learning*. Basil Blackwell.
Clements, S. and Griffiths, P. (1971) 'What is language across the curriculum? (Editorial)', *English in Education*, 5, 3-4.
Crystal, D. (1979) 'Language in education – a linguistic perspective', in Cashdan, A. (ed.) *Language, Reading and Learning*. Basil Blackwell.
DES (1975) *A Language for Life* (The Bullock report). HMSO.
DES (1984) *English from 5 to 16, Curriculum Matters 1*. HMSO.
Gillham, B. (ed.) (1985) *The Language of School Subjects* (In Press).
Lunzer, E. A. and Gardner, W. K. (1979) *The Effective Use of Reading*. Heinemann Educational.
Marland, M. (Ed.) (1977) *Language Across the Curriculum*. Heinemann Educational.
Moor, R. (1985) 'Language for learning at FE level'. *NATFHE Journal*, April, 34-5.
NATE (1976) *Language Across the Curriculum – Guidelines for Schools*. NATE/Ward Lock Educational.
Perera, K. (1984) *Children's Writing and Reading*. Basil Blackwell.
SED (1978) *The Education of Pupils with Learning Difficulties in Primary and Secondary Schools in Scotland*. HMSO.
Talk Workshop Group (1982) *Becoming Our Own Experts: The Vauxhall Papers*. Inner London Education Authority English Centre.
Torbe, M. (ed.) (1980) *Language Policies in Action*. Ward Lock Educational.
Wood, D., McMahon, L. and Cranstoun, Y. (1980) *Working With Under-Fives*. Grant McIntyre.

2

Styles of interaction and opportunities for learning

Gordon Wells

Introduction

In trying to answer the question 'where does a child's control of his or her native language come from?', two contrasting theoretical explanations have come to dominate discussion. On the one hand, there is the position expounded by Chomsky (1965, 1976), Lenneberg (1967) and McNeil (1966), which emphasises the autonomous nature of the child's construction of language. According to this account, the learning process is determined by the innate structure of the learner operating upon the specific organisation of whichever human language he or she is exposed to. An input of primary linguistic data is necessary, of course, but, provided it contains a proportion of well-formed sentences appropriate to their situational context, the precise form of the input does not significantly affect the course that learning takes.

The second explanation, by contrast, emphasises the role of the environment. Observations across a wide range of language communities show that adults when speaking to young language learners modify their speech in the direction of syntactic simplicity and semantic and pragmatic redundancy in context. These features, it is argued by Snow (1977), Rondal (1983) and others, provide the child with what is, effectively, graded instruction concerning the formal structure of the language and the way in which form is related to intended meaning. Some degree of structural pre-adaptation to the task on the part of the learner is assumed, of course, but in this account the main burden of explanation for the course taken in acquisition falls on the input.

The same sort of alternative explanations can also be brought to bear on the variation in educational attainment that is associated with social class, in so far as this is attributable to educational attainment. On the one hand, there are those who have argued that this variation is largely determined by inherited potential. On the other hand, others have claimed that the class-related variation that undoubtedly occurs is caused by differences in language use, which significantly affect children's ability to make use of the opportunities provided by formal education. According to this latter explanation, whether it be a matter of dialect (Labov, 1970) or sociolinguistic code (Bernstein, 1971), the disadvantage experienced by many lower-class children is said to be in their being inadequately prepared for the linguistic demands of the classroom by having learned a different model of language in use from their parents and the other members of their immediate language community.

Both Labov and Bernstein, quite rightly, question the appropriateness of the language demands that are made on such children in the schools they attend. Both also point out that 'different' does not mean 'less effective' when comparing the ways in which meaning intentions are given expression through grammatical forms, vocabulary and pronunciation. But, as with those who emphasise the tutoring role of the adult input in initial language learning, both these authors emphasise the influence of the environment on the repertoire of linguistic resources that the child masters as a result of interaction with members of the family circle.

To many, these theoretical accounts are mutually exclusive alternatives, with acceptance of either one requiring the rejection of the other. But this, I believe, is a mistake. A major reason for the apparent conflict is the tendency for scholars to focus, in their study of language, either on the internal structure of the language system or alternatively on the uses to which the resources of language are put in inter-personal communication. But surely it would be more appropriate to see the two perspectives as complementary. As Halliday (1984) points out, language is both system *and* resource. And, in learning their native language, children both participate in linguistic interaction to achieve their communicative purposes and draw on that experience in order to construct their representation of the rules – the grammar that underlies that interaction.

As far as the autonomy of the learner is concerned, this is attested by the child's construction of 'incorrect' transitional rules, in spite of the lack of supporting evidence in the input: for example, the early preference for fixed word order in languages where this is variable (Slobin, 1982); the well-known phenomenon of over-regularisation of irregular forms (e.g. 'goed', 'sheeps'); and the systematic 'errors' that Bowerman (1972) has observed in much older children. Evidence of a different kind is to be found in the fact that there is a very high degree of similarity between children in the sequence in which learning takes place, despite considerable variation in the range and quality of the language that is modelled in the utterances that individual children hear (Wells, 1985). This suggests a very high degree of similarity in the mental structure that is brought to bear on the input by language learners and in the strategies that they employ in constructing and progressively modifying their internal grammar.

Similarity of sequence in learning does not, however, imply similarity in rate of learning, or even in the level of mastery ultimately attained. Differences of this kind are both substantial and early to appear (Wells, 1982, 1985), and whilst no doubt partly attributable to differences in genetic endowment, they are almost certainly also due to differences in the opportunities for learning that are provided by children's linguistic environments.

Learning a language, as Halliday (1984) and Hymes (1971)

amongst others have pointed out, involves more than acquiring a grammatical system that will generate well-formed sentences. It involves learning how to produce and understand sentences in a wide variety of contexts, that is to say how to use language as a resource for communicating with other people. Sentences take on their meaning for an individual in relation to the situations in which they are used. Their effectiveness as a resource depends on the range of purposes to which the learner discovers they may be put from his or her experience of interaction with other speakers. The importance of the quality of this experience is beginning to emerge from a number of recent studies, which show that differences in language use by adults are significantly assoc-iated with variation in their children's rate of development (see Wells and Robinson, 1982, for a review).

The argument of this paper, therefore, is that language learning should be seen as resulting from an *interaction* between an organism pre-adapted to the learning task and an environment which, to varying degrees, facilitates that task by providing the evidence that the organism requires. However, learning is also dependent on interaction in another sense, for it is participation in conversation that provides learners with opportunities to construct and test their representation of language, both as system and as resource.

As educators, we are concerned with the characteristics of both learners and their environments. But most particularly we are concerned with the way in which learners and environments interact, for it is in that interaction that we, as parents and teachers, can best help children to realise their linguistic and intellectual potential by adopting a conversational style that maximises their opportunities for learning.

In the remainder of this paper, therefore, I shall review some of the evidence that is becoming available on adults' styles of interaction in the settings of home and school, and on the influences that these styles have on children's learning.

Styles of interaction in the home

The literature on the input to language learners is now quite extensive (cf. Snow (1977) and Wells and Robinson (1982) for reviews), almost all of it showing that adults systematically adjust their speech when talking with young children. Initially, the main aim of this research was to demonstrate the inaccuracy of Chomsky's characterisation of the input as 'random and degenerate' but, more recently, attempts have been made to show that particular features of this register actually facilitate the learner's task. Typically, discussion of the various features and their potential facilitation has been conducted in terms of the different linguistic levels involved: syntax, semantics and pragmatics. But, to date, no consensus has emerged about which is the most important.

In the light of the preceding discussion, however, I wish to suggest an alternative classification: one which is based on the intentions – albeit not necessarily conscious – that adults might have in modifying their speech in particular ways when talking to children. First, we can distinguish modifications that facilitate the child's access to the organisation of the language system: features such as simplicity of structure, well-formedness, clarity of pronunciation etc. Second, there are adjustments that have as their goal the achievement of mutual comprehension and, in particular, the adult's understanding of the child's intention. These are seen in the repetitions, checks, and expansions which are noted as so prominent in some parents' speech by Brown (Brown, Cazden and Bellugi, 1969) and Cross (1977). Third, we can distinguish certain adjustments that serve to encourage and support the child's participation in conversation. These would include such features as: allowing the child to initiate a high proportion of interactions: providing conversational bridges – 'turnabouts' as Kaye and Charney (1980) call them – which both respond to the child's previous utterance and invite him or her to say more; making reference predominantly

to the child's or to joint activities; and responding to the
child's utterances with extensions, which both confirm the
acceptability of his or her contribution and help them to
pursue the topic further. Finally, in contrast to the previous
characteristics, there are modifications which seem to have a
more didactic function: corrections, display questions and a
tendency on the part of the adult to initiate a high proportion
of topics, and to pursue them at the expense of the topics that
the child might wish to introduce.

Considered in these terms, the results of the various studies
are more consistent. Features of the first type are almost
universally found in adult speech to children, but in general
they are not found to be associated with variation in the
children's rate of learning (Newport, Gleitman and Gleitman,
1977; Cross, 1978; Ellis, 1978). As we have argued elsewhere
(Wells and Robinson, 1982), however, this should not be
taken as evidence against the facilitating effect of an input
containing clear, well-formed examples of the target language
at an appropriate level of complexity. In the first place, the
lack of significant correlations with regard to this group of
features may result from the limited variance observed in
most studies: apparently *all* adults make such adjustments
when speaking to young children. Second, it is not absolute
simplicity that is helpful in the input, but rather a tuning of
the degree of complexity to the child's stage of development
and to the on-going demands of the conversation.

Of the remaining three types of modification, it is the first
and second which have been found to be associated with
children's differential rates of progress (Cross, 1978; Ellis,
1978). In our own most recent study, which included features
corresponding to all three hypothesised intentions, significant
positive correlations were found between accelerated
development and a high frequency of expansions, extensions
and references to joint activities, whilst features corresponding to a didactic intention showed either no correlation or a
trend towards a negative association (Barnes et al., 1983;
Wells, 1985).

From the interactional perspective outlined above, this is what would be expected. Conversation is by its nature collaborative, depending on the establishment and maintenance of inter-subjectivity. Where one of the participants is less skilled in shaping and placing his or her contributions towards the joint construction of conversational meaning, strategies employed by the more mature participant which enable the novice to participate more fully will lead to conversations that are more mutually rewarding. This in turn will increase the child's motivation both to engage in further communication and to discover the means for realising his or her communicative intentions more adequately.

Styles of interaction in the classroom

At home, then, children are active learners, constructing their knowledge of language from their experience of language in use. And as they learn their native language, they also use language to learn other things. There is no curriculum, of course. Most of the learning that occurs does so spontaneously, as problems arise in everyday activities and are resolved, often with the help of an adult, who provides an additional resource of skill and knowledge.

Then at about the age of 5 years, children go to school, making a transition to a social environment which is very different from that of the home. Two factors in particular are responsible for the difference: first, the large number of children assigned to the care of a single adult and, second, the curricular aims which provide the framework for most of the activities that take place. Some 'culture shock' is inevitable but, ideally, one would hope to see every effort made to ease the transition. Opportunities for interaction with an adult will of necessity be reduced but, when they do occur, one would hope that, with the benefit of professional training, teachers would ensure these opportunities were at least as enabling as those that occur at home. Indeed, some educational theorists have claimed that, by comparison with many (particularly lower-class) homes, schools provide a much richer language environment, which can provide compensation for earlier linguistic deprivation.

Is this in fact the case? Both Tizard (Tizard et al., 1980) and Wood (Wood, McMahon and Cranstoun, 1980) have cast some doubt on this rosy view of the linguistic opportunities provided in nursery schools, but there has been no comparable study of infant schools in Britain. So, during the last two years, we have made a systematic comparison of the language experience of 32 five year olds, as they made the transition from home to school.

The children were selected from the representative sample studied in a previous phase of the Bristol Language Development Project and included an equal number of boys and girls drawn from the full range of family backgrounds. Recordings of spontaneous interaction were made, first at home a few weeks before starting school, and then in the classroom after approximately six weeks at school. In both settings nine 5-minute samples were recorded at 20-minute intervals between 9 a.m. and 12 noon, using a radio-microphone. No observer was present during the home observations but, for technical reasons, it was found necessary to have an observer in the classroom and, this being so, it was decided to introduce a video-recorder as well. However, probably because of the demonstration that preceded the classroom observations, the children completely ignored the researchers and their equipment, and there were no grounds for doubting the naturalness of their behaviour. The teachers, too, although undoubtedly aware of the presence of the researchers, gave no evidence of departing from their usual classroom routines. Presumably if they did modify their behaviour it was in the direction of approximating more closely to their own beliefs about what constitutes good teaching.

Unfortunately, some recorded samples were lost because

the children were outside in the playground or on excursions from the home, so when the recordings had been transcribed seven samples only were picked for analysis, a random procedure being used to make the selection where more than seven had been recorded. Every utterance was then coded with respect to the following categories: context of activity, speaker and addressee, communicative function, semantic content, temporal reference, syntactic complexity and incorporation (i.e. nature of the relationship with preceding utterances – this category was coded on adult utterances only). Coding was carried out by three coders, each child's home and school observations being coded by the same person. Inter-coder reliability ranged between 84 per cent and 89 per cent. Frequencies were then computed across contexts for each category in each observation and, for all adult-child interaction, a first-level comparison was made between the two settings of home and school, using the Z ratio of the difference between means. Subsequently, a three-way analysis of variance was carried out to investigate the relationship between setting, sex and class of family background.

As can be seen from table 2.1, the results of the first analysis are clear-cut and systematic. Compared with their experience at home, children at school play a much less active role in conversation. They initiate fewer interactions and fewer exchanges, ask fewer questions and make fewer requests. Their utterances are syntactically simpler, contain a narrower range of semantic content, and less frequently refer outside the here-and-now. Indeed, almost half their utterances are elliptical or moodless, often being minimal responses to requests for display. On the other hand, when contrasted with parents, teachers dominate conversation, initiating the majority of interactions and exchanges, predominantly through requests, questions and requests for display. They are also more than twice as likely to develop their own meanings as they are to extend those contributed by children, this ratio being almost the exact opposite of that found in the speech of parents.

*Table 2.1   Comparison of adult-child conversation at home
and school (n = 32)*

	Home	School	Significance level of difference
Absolute values			
Mean no. of child utterances to adults	122.0	45.0	$p < 0.001$
Mean no. of adult utterances to child	152.7	128.7	n.s.
Mean no. of child turns per interaction	4.1	2.5	$p < 0.001$
Mean child syntactic complexity	3.1	2.4	$p < 0.001$
Mean adult syntactic complexity	3.5	4.3	$p < 0.001$
Mean no. of categories of semantic content in child speech [a]	15.5	7.9	$p < 0.001$
Proportional values (percentages, child)			
Initiation of interaction	63.6	23.0	$p < 0.001$
Exchange-initiating utterances	70.2	43.8	$p < 0.001$
Complete statements	31.2	28.0	n.s.
Questions	12.7	4.0	$p < 0.001$
Requests	14.3	10.4	$p < 0.05$
Elliptical or moodless utterances	29.4	49.4	$p < 0.001$
Utterances in text-contingent exchanges	9.4	6.3	$p < 0.10$
References to non-present time	9.1	6.4	$p < 0.05$
Proportional values (percentages, adult)			
Exchange-initiating utterances	59.9	78.7	$p < 0.001$
Complete statements	26.2	24.5	n.s.
Questions	14.3	20.2	$p < 0.01$
Requests	22.5	34.1	$p < 0.001$
Elliptical utterances	5.7	5.8	n.s.
Requests for display	2.1	14.2	$p < 0.001$
Extending child's meaning	33.5	17.1	$p < 0.001$
Developing adult's meaning	19.3	38.6	$p < 0.001$

[a] For this comparison only, n = 16.

In sum, compared with homes, schools provide a significantly reduced opportunity for children to learn through talk with an adult, and in those conversations that do occur, children find themselves forced into the respondent role, their contributions for the most part only being valued if they contribute to the teacher's predetermined line of thought. The result is that they make less use of their linguistic resources than they do at home and have less opportunity to extend those they already possess, except perhaps in relation to the specific vocabulary associated with the tasks they are required to perform.

These results, confirming as they do those of Tizard et al. (1980) and Wood, McMahon and Cranstoun (1980) in relation to the nursery, must make us question the claims that schools provide a linguistically rich environment, able to provide compensation for children believed to be linguistically deprived at home. However, the results of the analysis of variance, like those of Tizard et al. (1980), produced little evidence that there really is a substantial difference between homes of different social classes in the quality of interaction that children experience with their parents. For only one variable was there a significant main effect: lower class children asked more questions than middle-class children, both at home and at school ($F = 6.47$, $p<0.05$). It appears, therefore, that there are very few homes that do not provide richer opportunities than are found at school for learning through interaction with adults.

Schools as environments for learning

The reasons for this situation are not far to seek. Teachers may give their verbal assent to such precepts as the need to 'start where the child is' and to 'individualise children's learning'. But under the increasing pressures imposed by larger classes, dwindling resources and the relentless demand for accountability, they find themselves adopting styles of classroom management that militate against the achievement of the aims they claim to espouse.

Of all these pressures, perhaps the most insidious is the emphasis on standardising the curriculum to ensure that all pupils master the basic skills. Clearly, it is highly desirable that every pupil should become literate and numerate and be conversant with certain basic facts about his or her social and physical environment. But these skills are only of value when they are integrated with the purposes and interests that the learner brings from outside the classroom. As Barnes (1976) puts it, to be useful, school knowledge must be converted into action knowledge.

Too often, however, the current concern with curriculum takes little account of what individual pupils bring to the tasks they are required to perform, concentrating instead on the specification of structured and graded teaching steps that will help to ensure that all pupils progress in a predetermined sequence towards a predetermined goal. The result is, as we have seen, a tendency towards a teacher-dominated style of interaction, in which children are placed in the passive role of respondents, obliged to accept the teacher's definition of what is considered relevant.

This is very different from the situation that obtains in the early stages of language learning. There, it was argued, the child is *actively* involved in the construction of knowledge, learning from others through the collaborative making of meaning. Although the emphasis gradually changes, as the child gets older, from learning the language system to using language as a resource to learn about other things, there is no reason to believe that there is an abrupt change at the point of entry to school in the learning strategies that the child employs, or in the characteristics of adult behaviour that provide the most help.

Apart from direct experience, talk with adults continues to be, potentially, the child's richest source of information about the world he or she lives in. Conversation can also provide them with one of the most effective means for trying out ideas and modifying them in the light of the feedback received. Of course, for conversation to provide opportunities for learning in this way, children must be encouraged to continue to be active participants, initiating talk about topics that interest them, asking questions and expressing their opinions. And the adults with whom they interact must continue to be interested in what they have to say, more concerned to answer questions and to sustain and extend their interests than to tell them what the adults think they ought to know and then to check that they can remember what they were told (Wood, 1983).

Our observations of 5-year-old children have shown us that, compared with parents, teachers are not very successful in fulfilling these requirements. Part of the reason for this is to be found in the constraints imposed by agencies outside the classroom. But part, I would suggest, is to be found in the conception that teachers have of what it is to be a teacher and that, in turn, depends on what they believe about the way in which children learn.

Some of the things that children need to learn can no doubt be mastered by drill and practice under the control of a teacher. But the argument of this paper has been that the most effective learning occurs when the child is allowed to take a more active role in the process. We need to see teaching, therefore, not as the transmission of pre-existing knowledge to passive recipients, but rather as the provision of opportunities for children to continue to exercise their in-built drive actively to make sense of their experience and, thereby, to gain understanding of, and control over, the world in which they live. Of course we shall want to ensure that their learning becomes more systematic and that their horizons are widened to encompass ways of thinking which they would not encounter if left to their own devices. But the aim must be to do this in a manner which allows scope for each individual child to share in the responsibility for initiating and carrying out the tasks through which learning takes place. In an important sense, therefore, teaching is best thought of as the guiding and facilitating of learning, and the style of interaction called for is one in which there is reciprocity and collaboration in the making of meaning.

Notes

An earlier version of this chapter was presented at the Third Language and Language Acquisition Conference, 'Pragmatics and Education', held in Ghent, Belgium in March, 1983.

The research is funded by the Social Science Research Council (SSRC) and the Nuffield Foundation, whose support is gratefully acknowledged. (For fuller details of the research and methodology see Wells 1981, 1982.)

References

Barnes, D. (1976) *From Communication to Curriculum*. Penguin.

Barnes, S.B., Gutfreund, M., Satterly, D. and Wells, C.G. (1983) 'Characteristics of adult speech which predict children's language development', *Journal of Child Language, 10*, 65-84.

Bernstein, B. (1971) *Class, Codes and Control*, vol. 1. Routledge & Kegan Paul.

Bowerman, M. (1982) 'Reorganizational processes in language development', in Wanner, E. and Gleitman, L.R. (eds), *Language Acquisition: the State of the Art*. Cambridge University Press.

Brown, R., Cazden, C. and Bellugi, U. (1969) 'The child's grammar from 1 to 111', in Hill, J.P. (ed.), *The 1967 Minnesota Symposium on Child Psychology*, vol. 2. University of Minneapolis Press.

Chomsky, N.A (1965) *Aspects of the Theory of Syntax*. MIT Press.

Chomsky, N.A. (1976). *Reflections on Language*. Temple Smith.

Cross, T.G. (1977) 'Mothers' speech adjustments: contribution of selected child listener variables', in Snow, C. E. and Ferguson, C. A. (eds), *Talking to Children*, Cambridge University Press.

Cross, T.G. (1978) 'Mothers' speech and its association with rate of linguistic development in young children', in Snow, C. and Waterson, N. (eds), *The Development of Communication*. Wiley.

Ellis, R.J. (1978) Enabling Factors in Caretaker-Child Discourse. Unpublished MEd. dissertation, University of Bristol School of Education.

Halliday, M.A.K. (1984) 'Language as code and language as behaviour: a systemic-functional interpretation of the nature and ontogenesis of dialogue', in Fawcett, R.P., Halliday, M.A.K., Lamb, S.M. and Makkai, A. (eds), *Semiotics of Culture and Language*. Francis Pinter.

Hymes, D. (1971) 'Competence and performance in linguistic theory', in Huxley, R. and Ingram, E. (eds), *Language Acquisition: Models and Methods*. Academic Press.

Kaye, K. and Charney, R. (1980) 'How mothers maintain 'dialogue' with two-year-olds', in Olson, D. (ed), *The Social Foundation of Language and Thought*. Norton.

Labov, W. (1970) 'The logic of non-standard English', in Williams, F. (ed), *Language and Poverty*. Markham.

Lenneberg, E.H. (1967) *Biological Foundations of Language*. Wiley.

McNeill, D. (1966). 'The creation of language by children', in Lyons, J. and Wales, R. (eds), *Psycholinguistics Papers*. University of Edinburgh Press.

Newport, E.L., Gleitman, H. and Gleitman, L.R. (1977) 'Mother I'd rather do it myself: some effects and non-effects of maternal speech style', in Snow, C.E. and Ferguson, C.A. (Eds), *Talking to Children: Language Input and Acquisition*. Cambridge University Press.

Rondal, I.A. (1983) *L'Interaction Adulte-Infant et la Construction du Langage*. Pierre Mordaga.

Slobin, D.I. (1982) 'Universal and particular in the acquisition of language', in Wanner, E. and Gleitman, L.R. (eds), *Language Acquisition: the State of the Art*. Cambridge University Press.

Snow, C. (1977) 'Mother's speech research: from input to acquisition', in Snow, C. E. and Ferguson, C. A. (eds), *Talking to Children*. Cambridge University Press.

Tizard, B., Carmichael, H., Hughes, M. and Pinkerton, G. (1980) 'Four year olds talking to mothers and teachers', in Hersov, L.A. et al. (eds), *Language and Language Disorders in Childhood*. Pergamon.

Wells, C.G. (1981) *Learning through Interaction: the Study of Language Development*. Cambridge University Press.

Wells, C.G. (1982) *Language, Learning and Education*. Centre for the Study of Language and Communication, University of Bristol, School of Education.

Wells, C.G. (1985) *Language Development in the Pre-School Years*. Cambridge University Press.

Wells, C.G. and Robinson, W.P. (1982) 'The role of adult speech in Language Development', in Fraser, C. and Scherer, K. (eds), *The Social Psychology of Language*. Cambridge University Press.

Wood, D. (1983) 'Teaching: natural and contrived', *Child Development Society Newsletter*, *31*, 2–7.

Wood, D., McMahon, L. and Cranstoun, Y. (1980), *Working with Under Fives*. Grant McIntyre.

3

Cognitive processes in reading and spelling

Geoffrey and Jean Underwood

Skilled reading depends upon a flexibility in the application of component subskills, and so it is with all skills. A chess Grand Master is aware not only of the current state of the board but of past positions and of the probability of any future move. He or she does not need to look ponderously at each piece on the board to be sure whether it is a pawn or a king. Pieces are not seen only as individuals, but also as parts of larger patterns. The movement of certain pieces is anticipated, and sequences of movements integrated into overall impressions of the progress of the game. Perhaps the most important characteristic of an expert chess player, however, is flexibility when uncertainty arises. When expectations are violated, recognition of the new position must be accurate, and the new pattern of relationships analysed. In terms of the principles involved, we could be talking here about playing chess or reading a page of text. For the beginning reader uncertainty will occur over the identity of individual letters and words, but the flexible interaction of different sources of information will help solve recognition problems. Flexibility of process is a characteristic of individual development, and is a main theme of this chapter. The second theme concerns the importance of developing automatic word-recognition skills so that attention can be released for comprehension calculations.

The discussion is biased towards the cognitive processes involved during reading, with spelling considered as an adjunct which uses (and misuses) some of the same processes. This bias is partly by design, and partly a reflection of the amount of research conducted upon the two activities. Another bias is in the emphasis on recognition processes, rather than linguistic and comprehension ones. A number of sources of research reviewed here suggest that the major differences between good and poor readers of all ages are in word-decoding processes, and that the surest way of improving an individual's reading ability is to improve their sight vocabulary. With these biases declared, the discussion starts by setting reading into the general theoretical context of the flow of information through an individual's cognitive processes.

Reading as an information processing skill

Models of those cognitive processes involved in reading and spelling emphasise the available sources of information, and the related transformational processes necessary to convert a visual symbol into a spoken utterance or an understanding of an idea. We shall preface our discussion with a few remarks about the nature of information and about the transformations which are undertaken in the mind of the skilled reader. This analysis of cognitive processes will proceed by reference to differences between skilled and unskilled readers, not because our main concern is with disability, but because individual differences serve to illustrate the nature of ability.

Text can be described technically as information, in that information is that which eliminates uncertainty. As information is extracted from the page the reader becomes less uncertain about the letters, words and meanings which it contains. In the course of understanding print, the reader may be said to *process* or *transform* the information from a visual code to a semantic code. When reading aloud, for instance, a

visual analysis will be followed by a transformation into a
sound-based code, and the process in this case may involve
the application of grapheme-to-phoneme correspondence
(GPC) rules. These are the formal rules by which the
graphemes which form words are translated into the code
used for pronunciation. The graphemes themselves are
individual letters or small groups of letters such as 'b', 'ou',
and 'ght', and when we can identify these graphemes and then
pronounce them together as the sound represented by /bo:t/
(which rhymes with 'port'), we can be said to have used the
GPC rules. Applying the rules to information available in a
graphemic code will result in processing into a phonological
code. In this case, 'application of the GPC rules' is a cognitive
process, and we can determine the extent to which skilled
readers use this process by experiments that manipulate
words which do and do not obey the rules. In the case of
spelling, the transformation is from the spoken code for a
word to the graphemic code, and the process selected can
similarly render a correct or incorrect code. In describing
reading as an information-processing skill it is necessary to
identify the sources of information and the cognitive processes applied to that information, and to indicate how these
sources and processes vary as the skill develops. First we shall
outline the implications of describing reading as a skill.

Component subskills in reading and spelling

A characteristic feature of any skill is a hierarchical organisation of component subskills. The skill of writing comprises
components which include an ability to hold the pen or
pencil, an ability to form letters of the alphabet and to join
them into recognisable words and sentences, and so on. It is
necessary to learn each of these activities in order to be able to
write, and this learning process occurs only with practice.
During learning, and particularly during the early stages of

learning, writers will need to think continuously about their movements and about the response of the pen to those movements. When they know how the pen will respond they no longer need to think about it, and will eventually be unaware of skilful minor corrective movements. The activity will then become flexible, in that performance will be unaffected by differences between writing instruments and between writing surfaces. The component subskills can then be described as being automatised – the movements occur as the position of the pen demands them, without the writer having consciously to calculate them. Control of the activity will have then passed from the awareness of the performer and attention will be released for higher-level activities. In the case of writing these might include grammatical style and the choice of a topic of composition. The skill can be described as a group of inter-related subskills which do not require moment-by-moment attention, and this is also an appropriate description of skilled reading. These notions of the automatis-ation of processes which no longer require close monitoring are described in more detail in Underwood (1982), but for the present purposes it is sufficient to note that attention can only be devoted to higher-level activities, such as comprehension, when lower-level activities have become skilled through practice.

The subskills themselves are not the purpose of the activity, but they must be developed to serve the needs of the higher-level complex activity. The higher-level activity itself can, of course, become automatised, and whereas in the case of skills such as riding a bicycle or tying shoelaces this is advantageous, when it happens to writing or reading the consequences are unfortunate. Automatised writing – writing while one's thoughts are elsewhere – is relatively rare. Automatised reading is something that most of us have experienced, however. When the components are well-practised, control passes to a higher level of organisation, and with reading, as we shall be arguing later, the highest level is the integration of word meanings in a comprehension 'calculation'. If we choose not to attend to the higher-level activity during cycling we simply do not notice our surroundings and may take an incorrect route. The equivalent during reading is having our eyes arrive at the bottom of the page without the slightest understanding of what the author had intended. This is not a failure to understand resulting from the difficulty of the material, but from attention being on matters other than the content of the text. If we daydream while going through the motions of reading we can still recognise words, and perhaps even convince ourselves that we are reading. The letters and words will be recognised – they are handled by automatised component subskills – but the meanings of the words are not assembled into the ideas which the author has attempted to express. This is an activity which cannot become automatised, and unless the reader's attention is directed towards the underlying meanings of sentences the author's ideas cannot be calculated. Briefly, this is because automatisation depends upon practice at performances which do not vary, whereas the underlying meanings of sentences are very rarely the same. Words almost always have constant meaning, for without this property they would have little use. Once words are grouped together in sentences, however, a range of ideas are conveyed, and this depends upon the combinations and juxtapositions of those words.

Having described the assumptions of the approach, we shall now describe the cognitive processes necessary for skilled reading and spelling, emphasising the subskills involved in word recognition, anticipation, and integration.

Decoding processes in single word recognition and production

The recognition of a word during reading is the process by which a purely visual stimulus is understood as the symbol for a specific meaning. The problem for beginning readers is to decode the visual symbols into a form which can be recognised, for it is only then that they will be able to bring previously gained knowledge to bear upon the meaning of the text.

Suppose you are reading in poor light, and that you glance at a word for long enough to identify the letters 'comme£ce'. The £ represents an unidentified letter, so is the word 'commence' or 'commerce'? Careful inspection of the doubtful letter will allow the use of further visual information, and the difference between the 'n' and the 'r' will permit final word recognition. In this case, visual information will have been used as the basis of a decision, and a decision is necessary because English orthography allows one of two letters in this position in our target word. If the letters 'commenc£' had been identified, then the remaining letter would not be in doubt, at least for the skilled reader. Orthographic knowledge would combine with extracted visual information to allow only one completion, and so the identification of further visual features would be redundant.

The use of this example does not condone the parody of reading as 'guessing'. As Goodman (1976) and Smith (1978) have pointed out, information is richly available on the printed page, and there are a number of ways of determining the identity of a letter or word. The skilled reader does not guess so much as eliminate alternatives by the most efficient route. As more alternatives are rejected, the value of the information increases. In this description of text as information, it is necessary to describe the features which are used in deciding what meanings are being conveyed.

Visual information does not only come in the form of specific letter identification. If the unidentified letters had been 'shar£' then a number of words could have been presented. However, if the overall shape of the word had indicated a descending letter in the terminal position, then only one common word is possible. Shape information alone is only occasionally sufficient to identify a word, but in conjunction both with other information and with orthographic knowledge, it can be useful. Skilled readers are disturbed when word shape is eliminated as a cue, especially when cAsE iS aLtErNaTeD. When words are printed in upper-case letters alone they have reduced shape information, and are more difficult to recognise than those printed in lower-case. When they are put into the context of a congruent sentence, however, this disadvantage is reduced (Underwood and Bargh, 1982), suggesting that two sources of information, context and word shape, can be used in combination by practised readers.

The grammatical and semantic context of presentation of a word is often sufficient to identify words, and in the context:

The deep sea fisherman found a shar£

there is no uncertainty, unless the sentence continues, as in:

The deep sea fisherman found a shar£ knife.

In the second sentence, which has a grain of ambiguity, grammar and meaning do not provide sufficient information for us to neglect the visual analysis. As the environment of a letter changes, so will the processes necessary for its analysis. The flexibility of reliance upon different sources of information is the hallmark of the successful reader.

How is the visual form of a word decoded into a meaningful token, and how are these tokens recoded into their visual forms during writing? Two component subskills, both involving relationships between print and meaning, are important in both reading and spelling. These subskills are (a) the analysis of visual patterns, and (b) the conversion of the written form of a word into a phonological form. These two processes are implemented in reading as word recognition via a purely graphemic route or via a phonological route, and they are also implemented as spelling by reliance upon visual pattern and by reliance upon phonetic pattern.

An appreciation of orthographic knowledge

There are, as we have already suggested, a number of sources of information available to the skilled reader. In addition to a simple visual analysis of the print, we can use our knowledge of orthography to guide this analysis. Letters regularly occur in certain combinations and positions with, for example, the letter Q always being followed by U, and a number of letters rarely appearing at the end of a word (e.g., J, V). Orthographic content is estimated by a tedious but accurate procedure by which a count is made of the number of times each letter appears in each position in a word of specific length. The letter O, for instance, does not occur very often as the final letter in a four letter word, but is common as the second letter. A word with letters in uncommon positions is regarded as having low orthographic redundancy, and this is sometimes described as low spatial redundancy. (Counts can be made of the occurrence of individual letters in specific word positions, and of pairs or triplets of letters, when estimating the spatial redundancy of a word.) Words such as 'card' and 'basket' have a higher spatial redundancy than words such as 'also' and 'action'. Experimental data show that skilled readers readily use their orthographic knowledge when processing words. In a very simple study of the use made of orthographic knowledge, Mason (1978) had adult readers name words or novel strings of letters forming 'nonwords' which varied in orthographic redundancy. It was found that words were named faster (i.e., the task was easier) when they had high spatial redundancy, and the same was true for nonsense nonwords created specifically for the experiment (e.g., 'cird' and 'bosket', in contrast with 'ilso' and 'abtion').

A further result from Mason's experiment, involving a flexibility in the use of different sources of information in readers of differing ability, is also of interest. Skilled adults could use one source of information to offset the adverse effects of another source, whereas unskilled adults showed cumulative adverse effects. Long, easy nonwords gained responses from the skilled readers which were no slower than those to short, difficult nonwords. For the poorer reader, however, increasing the word length always slowed the response time, with little assistance from the orthography. It is also of significance that Mason's effects were most apparent with novel strings of letters. Increasing the number of letters and decreasing the orthographic redundancy both served to make nonwords harder to pronounce, but this effect was less noticeable with true words. The nonwords should be thought of as new words, previously unencountered, and as letter-strings which could be words. The pronunciation of words was relatively unaffected by Mason's manipulations, possibly because skilled readers are able to use a variety of pronunci-ation strategies. For example, Glushko (1979) suggests that words are pronounced 'by analogy' with similar words – when deciding how to pronounce the letter-string 'fomily', comparison would be made with words of similar orth-ography. Indeed, in Mason's experiment, the skilled readers showed smaller overall response time differences between words and nonwords. When faced with familiar letter-strings in novel combinations, skilled readers perform better than less skilled readers.

Using the internal lexicon

An orthographic analysis is not the only way of recognising and pronouncing a string of letters. Words might also gain easier pronunciation as a result of having meanings. These meanings are considered to be organised in a cognitive system equivalent to a word memory or internal dictionary, which is called the lexicon. (It turns out that there may be a number of lexicons used by the skilled reader – for input and output processing, and for input of words by sight or sound – but for our purposes it is sufficient to talk of the lexicon as the store of word meanings. The discussion by Morton (1980) provides an advanced treatment of this notion of multiple lexicons.) The internal lexicon is the store of word memories, and for every word we can recognise there exists an entry in our personal lexicon. Some words occur in natural language more often than others, and these high-frequency words are recognised more readily than others, according to a number of measures. A thorough review of this literature, by Jastrzembski (1981), discusses the implications of the effects of frequency and number of meanings for this model of an internal lexicon. The lexicon notion explains the word frequency phenomenon by assuming that each entry has a *threshold* for recognition, and that recognition occurs only when sufficient data have been collected about the word for this threshold to be exceeded. When we know what a printed word is, we may be said to have collected data about it from the page. Some words have more stringent thresholds than others, and therefore require the collection of more data before we can be sure what we have seen. On the other hand, very common words are easily recognised – their lexical representations indicate recognition with the use of less data. Thresholds are not fixed, of course, and will vary greatly during the course of a lifetime. (How easily are the words 'micro' and 'monetarism' recognised in contemporary society, in contrast with their usage five or ten years ago?)

If the visual pattern on the page could contact the lexicon directly, without an intermediate orthographic analysis or GPC-decoding process, then the reader could pronounce the word on the basis of knowledge stored in the lexicon. The rules of pronunciation would not be available before recognition of the word and its meaning, unlike the GPC-pronunciation strategy. The GPC strategy is particularly useful when we need to pronounce unusual words such as 'leonine', 'potamic', or 'tachistoscope' – words which are slightly unfamiliar visually, and which may have a weak lexical representation. There are certain words which cannot be pronounced using the GPC route, however, and these are words with irregular grapheme-to-phoneme correspondences. Words such as 'both', 'pint', and 'steak' become unrecognisable if pronounced according to the GPC rules (they would rhyme with 'moth', 'mint', and 'meek'), and irregular words such as 'bread', 'come', and 'wild' actually become different words when pronounced according to these rules (i.e., 'breed', 'comb', and 'willed'). Knowing when *not* to apply the rules is clearly an important skill to acquire. Some words cannot be pronounced at all until their meaning has been recognised. These are the homographs such as 'invalid', 'refuse', and of course 'read', which have the same orthographic structure to represent a number of meanings. Each meaning has its own pronunciation, and so the lexicon must be consulted before the appropriate pronunciation can be construed. The correct meaning is presumably determined by using the semantic context of the sentence containing the homograph, but problems can still arise. Try reading the following passage aloud before continuing with the discussion. How does it make sense?

> There were neat and silent arrangements of column upon column of eager soldiers. Rows in the beer tent were quickly suppressed by the militia. The loud arguments were about short measures.

Of course, the ambiguous 'rows' could be interpreted either way in this example, but the most parsimonious reading is in the context of 'arguments'. One meaning is biased by the proximity of 'column', but whichever meaning is selected its pronunciation will *depend upon* interpretation, rather than precede it. The rules for pronunciation are therefore not necessarily used prior to the generation of possible meanings. It can be argued, it must be admitted, that when we come across one of these heterophonic homographs we generate all possible pronunciations before accessing the lexicon, and select the appropriate pronunciation on the basis of the derived meaning. Not only would this be inefficient and therefore slow, but introspection suggests that only rarely do we consciously ponder the pronunciations of words.

A further problem in relying upon GPC rules for lexical

access is encountered when we attempt to read words which are homophones. Some words *sound* like other words, even though they are orthographically dissimilar – an example would be the series 'seas', 'sees', and 'seize', all of which are pronounced as /se:z/ and rhyme with 'please'. If the phonological code of a homophone is used to access the lexicon, without reference to the spelling, then the wrong word could easily be identified. Even when we use the GPC rules this must be in conjunction with a maintained orthographic code of the word being processed.

So far, we have discussed ways in which different kinds of words may be pronounced using a range of cognitive processes. Words which are orthographically regular have at least three routes: the GPC route which uses orthographic components to derive their phonological correlates; the lexical route which uses the visual representation of the word to access meaning before generating the pronunciation; and Glushko's (1979) 'analogy' route whereby words can be pronounced in the same way as their orthographic associates. Orthographically irregular words cannot use the GPC route, and will fail by the analogy route if there is a mismatch between the regularity of the word and its associate (if you don't know how to pronounce 'have', you shouldn't try matching it with 'save'). The use of these routes can be demonstrated in simple laboratory experiments which measure the time taken to start pronouncing single words. Orthographically irregular words are pronounced more slowly than regular words (Baron and Strawson, 1976; Underwood and Bargh, 1982), indicating that they are treated differently in some way when they are read. The pronunciation of nonwords such as 'nouch' can be biased by the earlier presentation of either 'touch' or 'couch' (Kay and Marcel, 1981), suggesting that the analogy route can be used on occasions. When new words are encountered, either the GPC route or the analogy route may be used, but given the inconsistencies of English, neither route will ensure the correct pronunciation.

Using the GPC rules in reading and spelling

Given the variety of strategies available to us for the
pronunciation of words, it is not surprising that there are
marked individual differences in the ways in which skilled
readers respond to different kinds of words. Baron and
Strawson (1976) reported on the ways in which regular and
irregular words were processed by two general groups whom
they called 'Chinese' and 'Phoenician' readers. Individuals
who preferred the Chinese strategy are characterised as those
who recognise words as wholes, and who would use lexical
knowledge when checking spellings. The Phoenicians on the
other hand have a good knowledge of the GPC rules and
would use their othographic knowledge when looking for
incorrect spellings. Adults were allocated to one of these two
groups by a pair of tests which determined both GPC
familiarity and spelling ability before they were asked to
pronounce lists of regular or irregular words. A clear result
showed that it was the Phoenician readers who were most
vulnerable to the presence of irregular words. If an individual
relies upon word-decoding skills and spelling-to-sound correspondences when reading, then the appearance of words
which disobey the GPC rules will cause disruption. Individuals who use the lexical route for word recognition will
not suffer this interference, but they will not necessarily be
able to determine that a spelling is incorrect provided that the
word *sounds* acceptable.

The adult reader's use of a repertoire of cognitive processes
reflects the different occasions on which words are encountered, and the different kinds of words which exist in English
orthography. If the three routes are to be made available to a
beginning reader then two main types of skills will be
required – those involving the application of the GPC rules,
and the use of an extensive sight vocabulary. Skills depend for
their application upon knowledge, and there is no substitute
for practice in the development of a skill. Knowledge of the
GPC rules, and a familiarity with the shapes of letters and

words, are both essential. Dogmatic training techniques using only phonics or only sight vocabulary will result in restricted flexibility, and the processing of new or unfamiliar words will be impeded. Because the GPC route imposes a stage of processing between the visual analysis and the lexicon, it is necessarily slower in use than the direct lexical route. It is certainly used, however, and there are some indications that the acquisition of reading skills is associated with the appreciation of GPCs.

In a demonstration of the use of phonological coding, Barron (1978) had 11 year old and 12 year old children make yes/no decisions about the lexical status of letter-strings. In this 'lexical decision task' words gain a 'yes' response and nonwords a 'no'. It is a well-established phenomenon that nonwords which *sound* like actual words (known as 'pseudo-homophones') tend to gain slower responses than those which look as if they may be words, but do not sound like any. Slower decisions are made to nonwords such as 'burd' and 'phace' rather than those like 'deve' and 'slist', even though all four are word-like and could conceivably be words. It is important to note that all four can be pro-nounced, even though the lexical decision task does not require pronunciation, and is usually conducted in silence using finger response buttons. This effect can only arise if the nonwords are being transformed into a phonological code before lexical access is attempted. When the phonological code of 'phace' meets the entry for 'face' in the lexicon, a delay is imposed while the spelling is checked before initiation of the 'no' response. The appearance of the pseudohomophone effect is an indication of the application of the GPC rules to the letter-string as part of the processing strategy in this task. Barron found that pseudohomophones, unlike other nonwords, impaired the performance of good readers more than that of poor readers. The association between reading skill and the use of the GPC route was confirmed by a negative correlation between the time taken to pronounce a list of words and the size of the pseudohomophone impairment: the more skilled children gave a greater indication of being slowed down by the appearance of nonwords which sounded like words. It should perhaps be noted, however, that the advantage for phonological coding is not always shown by good readers. In experiments using British schoolchildren of the same age as Barron's, selected according to similar criteria for being classified as 'good' or 'poor' readers, we have found that on a variety of tasks the poorer readers do show an ability to use the phonological codes for printed words (Briggs and Underwood, 1982; Underwood and Briggs, 1984).

The use of the direct route to the lexicon, the route which uses the visual code of the word to access its lexical representation, can be demonstrated in a number of ways. Our ability to recognise words which violate the spelling-to-sound rules is in itself a demonstration that we do not always use the GPC route; but a simple experiment can also serve this purpose. Barron and Baron (1977) had children of a variety of ages compare a word with a picture to make either a rhyming decision or a meaning decision. On some occasions they made a response if the word and picture name sounded similar; otherwise they decided whether the two stimuli were related in meaning. The children performed these tasks either silently or while engaging in a task designed to suppress their vocalisation of the word names. The task was to repeat the words 'double, double, double' over and over again, and it was used on the assumption that, while vocalising, judgements about words would not be made on the basis of their phonological codes. Vocalisation suppression interfered with rhyming judgements in the experiment, but there was little interference with the meaning-similarity task. This suggests that even young children can use the lexical route to access the meaning of a printed word. A more extensive experiment conducted by Kleiman (1975) confirms this result for skilled readers. Vocalisation suppression impaired rhyming judgements, but had a reduced effect upon meaning judgements and visual-similarity judgements.

Although words can be processed by a number of different routes, for skilled readers the lexical route is the most attractive. Having no involvement with the GPC rules, it is a faster process, but it depends upon a large sight vocabulary. If the recognition skills are not well-developed, then the decoding process may have to take the more indirect route, employing the mediating phonological stage. There are other reasons for using the phonological code, either before or after word recognition has been obtained, and some which go towards explaining its extensive use include:

1 allowing the generation of a memory of what has been read,
2 imposing an intonation upon the print in the service of comprehension,
3 imposing an external control on the reader's attention to help convert the two-dimensional spatial display of text into a form appreciated by our temporally one-dimensional conscious processes.

Unless we read quickly, however, the integration of words in the sentence will suffer. This emphasises the importance of a large sight vocabulary which does not depend upon the application of the GPC rules for recognition. Comprehension depends upon the reader's ability to remember all the words in the sentence, and to integrate their meanings. The rapid recognition of word meanings will aid this process because earlier words will have had less opportunity for loss through forgetting.

Individual differences in spelling processes

Whereas word recognition is dependent upon a flexible use of a number of subskills, principally rapid visual processing and the selective use of phonological decoding as circumstances demand it, word production is more dependent upon the inflexible use of specific linguistic subskills. The orthography of the written output should not vary, of course, and a reliance upon the phonological codes of words can be positively misleading.

Poor spelling is often, but not always, associated with poor reading. Poor readers have a tendency to produce spelling errors which are non-phonological in that the sound structure of the intended word is not well represented in the error (see Camp and Dolcourt, 1977; Frith, 1979). Such errors may result from a failure to identify the appropriate grapheme (e.g., 'whose' → 'hows', and 'straight' → 'strat'), or a failure to segment the appropriate phoneme correctly (e.g., 'except' → 'exersept', and 'vehicle' → 'vercal'). At least some of these errors may be due in part to individual differences in dialect and incorrect pronunciation, but these four examples were produced in response to correctly spoken words in a spelling test. Learning to spell may well depend upon an ability to use phonological decoding strategies during reading, for the skilled use of the GPC rules will result in an awareness of the relationships between spelling and sound. An extensive use of these relationships will lead to an excess of spellings which are phonologically acceptable but orthographically incorrect. If we rely upon the sound of a word when attempting to spell, then errors will range from the gross 'autograph' → 'outergraff' to the more subtle 'honest' → 'onist'. Phonological spelling errors are often characteristic of good readers who are extending their use of the phonological strategy into an inappropriate task. Frith (1980) has suggested that these good readers attempt to 'spell by ear', in that they rely too heavily upon the phonological representations of words when it is more appropriate to use orthographic rules with a purely visual spelling check. Their word-recognition skills are so finely developed that they may take insufficient notice of orthography while reading, and so develop poor memories of how words are constructed when it comes to spelling them. Perin (1983) has recently reported that good readers who are poor spellers have just as much of a problem with phonetic segmentation as do poor readers. In estimating the number of phonemes in spoken versions of words such as 'autumn' and 'session' both groups of poor spellers made more errors than a group of good spellers, regardless of whether or not they were good readers. This result can be interpreted in support of Frith's contention, in that good readers who are poor spellers are those who do not have a good awareness of the relationships between sound and spelling.

Anticipation in sentence processing

The notion of an internal lexicon is particularly powerful in that it helps to explain many of the phenomena associated with word recognition. We have seen how the three strategies of recognition involve the lexicon in different ways, and differences in the processing of words can be best explained by reference to this notion. We have seen how entries in the internal lexicon can be more easily or less easily accessed according to whether they correspond to words which have a high or low frequency of occurrence in language. The ease of lexical access can also vary on a moment-to-moment basis as the context of the preceding sentence constrains the number of likely alternatives. Very common words, and particularly the short common words, are recognised so readily that we do not always look at them when reading text. It is all too easy to daydream while reading and thereby not recognise words which we are looking at, but it is also possible to recognise words which we are not looking at. The skipping of words during reading could result directly from rapid recognition of high-frequency words, or from the use of peripheral vision, but most likely from a combination of both of these factors. This section of the discussion concerns the use of sentence contexts in the recognition of words, and the way in which our eyes inspect some words in preference to others.

When does context aid word recognition?

A word presented at the end of a sentence is considerably easier to recognise than that same word presented in isolation.

This is one of the well-established results which Morton (1969) used in his influential model of the lexicon, which suggests that words become finally recognised when sufficient 'data' about them have been collected from the environment. The context provided by the sentence is considered by this model to be valuable as recognition data. The word itself provides visual data, of course, and the sentence provides contextual data which is of use only to individuals familiar with the syntax of the particular language in use. One might also predict that context would be of most use to individuals who have acquired rapid word-recognition skills and who can integrate word meanings rapidly. Such individuals, who would be described as good readers, are able to use the preceding context to reduce the number of possible words which could occur at the end of the sentence, making use of many sources of information and not relying exclusively upon any one source. This is the popular view of reading suggested by Goodman (1976) and Smith (1978), but it has a serious flaw. The flaw was uncovered in a straightforward experiment reported by West and Stanovich in 1978, in which children of different ages recognised words presented in the context of a sentence. Children read incomplete sentences such as 'the dog ran after the . . .', and as they finished pronouncing the final word, which was always the word 'the', a completing word was presented. This word was also to be read aloud, and the time taken to start pronouncing it was recorded. In the case of the sentence above, the completing word was 'cat', but on other trials a poor completion such as 'chair' was presented, so as to obtain an estimate of the effectiveness of the preceding context. To distinguish between the facilitating effects of useful context and the interfering effects of incongruous context, a third condition was incorporated. In this 'control' condition, only the word 'the' preceded the completing word, and West and Stanovich describe this as being a neutral context. According to the 'psycholinguistic guessing game' view of reading the good readers should make more use of the context than the poor readers, and in comparison with the neutral context they should perhaps show greater facilitation effects from congruous context and greater interference from the incongruous context. The opposite results were obtained, with the older readers showing smaller use of the context than the younger readers.

In a subsequent longitudinal study which observed the development of 7 year old children, Stanovich, West and Feeman (1981) found that the effects of context diminished as reading experience increased. These experiments do not support the notion that poor readers are unlikely to use context when reading, and go some way to suggesting that it is the poor readers who rely on context to aid their weak word-recognition skills. The good readers, in contrast, seem to recognise words so quickly that the beneficial (or harmful) effects of context do not have time to take effect. If word recognition is completed before the context can be used to generate a prediction, then the context would not be expected to have much of an effect upon the word, and more experienced readers do appear to be less influenced by context.

One conclusion which can be drawn from the Stanovich and West experiments on the effects of context is that the mark of a good reader is rapid word recognition. Good readers appear to be those who have good decoding skills and who have practised recognising words until they do not need to think about them. Using the terminology of 'information-processing skills', these readers have automatised an invariant process by practice, and the recognition of words becomes a component subskill. When this happens, attention does not need to be directed to decoding and it can be released for the integration of word meanings. For 'reading for meaning' to occur it is necessary for recognition to become automatised through practice, because until the reader no longer spends time thinking about the identity of individual words, he or she will not be able to think about their role in the sentence. Just as our Grand Master thinks about the manipulation of chess pieces, rather than about the identity of the pieces themselves, so the skilled reader thinks about manipulating word meanings and not about the identity of individual words.

Automatic word recognition during reading

Beginning readers need to acquire word-recognition skills so that they can spend their reading time thinking about the meanings of sentences rather than the meanings of words. West and Stanovich's (1978) experiment is important in suggesting that skilled readers are less affected by the context in which a word appears than are unskilled readers: younger readers may have to rely upon sentence contexts *because* their word-recognition skills are undeveloped. This is not to say that contexts are not used at all by adults, for word recognition is aided by context prior to a word and immediately after the word. Underwood, Whitfield and Winfield (1982) had adults read out a briefly presented word which followed a spoken and incomplete sentence. Congruous sentences gave faster word naming times than incongruous sentences, as might be expected, but this result was confounded by the appearance of a word printed to one side of the named word. This distractor word was printed in the position where the reader's eyes might next fixate the page if they were free to do so. As it was, the words were displayed too briefly to allow an eye movement during presentation. What we found was that distractors which appeared to the immediate right of the named word, and which fitted in the context of the sentence, tended to aid the naming of congruous words, and retard the naming of incongruous words. Our skilled readers appeared to be recognising the distractors even though they did not look at them, because their meanings influenced performance on the reading task.

This study of the effectiveness of words ahead of fixation confirms the West and Stanovich (1978) view of automatic word recognition, in that the distractor words were not attended to and were therefore read unintentionally. It goes further, and suggests that skilled readers recognise the meanings of words ahead of fixation. This might be of benefit in the construction of the meaning of the sentence, or it might be useful in helping to decide where to look next on the page. Our eyes do not wander randomly around the page when we are reading, but certain sorts of words are fixated more often than others (O'Regan, 1979), and this means that we must know in advance of a fixation where it is that we are going to look next. From the investigation of distracting unattended words we can conclude that words are recognised before they are fixated, and that meanings might be useful in guiding our eyes efficiently across the text. If this is the case, then it suggests that an important aspect of skilled reading is to avoid attending too closely to what is being fixated at any one moment, and to allow our eyes to be attracted to nearby interesting meanings.

The integration of word meanings

Comprehension is being presented here as an integration problem. As the words of a sentence are being recognised, using their orthographic structure, their sentence context or whatever, then they must be pieced together to reconstruct the underlying meaning of the sentence. Whereas word recognition can occur without the skilled reader thinking about it, sentence reconstruction cannot, and it is to this component subskill that the reader's attention should be directed. The lower-level subskills involved in word recognition can become automatised through practice, and this is necessary so that the reader's mind can be left free to attempt alternate integrations in order to calculate the writer's intended meaning. It is perfectly possible for the lower-level subskills to produce an activity which resembles reading, but without attention integration will not be possible. One example of this 'sham reading' is brought to our notice when we realise, on reaching the bottom of a page, that we have not been thinking about what the text means. Upon re-reading we know that we have seen the words before. This is because they have been processed automatically; but if our attention is on our own thoughts rather than the author's, then comprehension will fail.

A second example will be familiar to anyone who reads stories to children on a regular basis. Words can not only be recognised without attending to them, but they can also, with practice, be read aloud and whole sentences, and even passages, can be read with intonation. This is especially easy if the passage contains no uncommon words and is composed of sentences with predictable structure, for automatic performance depends upon a simple informational input. Books such as those used for beginning readers are useful for demonstrating this effect, and if you have found yourself daydreaming or thinking about a conversation with a colleague while 'going through the motions' of reading to a child, this does not mean that your reading was inadequate. A characteristic of automatic performance is an apparent loss of memory for what has been done during the previous few moments. This can happen while driving a car over a familiar route, and it can happen while reading predictable passages of text. It simply indicates that the focus of attention is our thoughts rather than our external environment. Highly predictable passages – those with little information in them – can be read aloud without attention, but books such as this one require the reader to think about the meanings of the sentences.

The automatic recognition of word meanings has been demonstrated in a number of experimental investigations. The usual procedure is to divert the reader's attention to one task, and observe the influence of an unattended word upon the reader's performance. If the meaning of the unattended word is critical in demonstrating an effect, then we can conclude that attention is not necessary for the recognition of word meanings, and this argument was used in the experiment by Underwood, Whitfield and Winfield (1982) described above. A related procedure was used by Kleiman (1975); we have also briefly mentioned his experiment in our earlier discussion of using the GPC rules in reading and spelling. Kleiman divided his readers' attention between an auditory task and a word-judgement task, to investigate the interfering effect of one upon the other. The auditory task consisted of listening to a random list of numbers and repeating them as they were presented. The list was continuous, and so it was not a matter of waiting until the end before repeating the numbers from memory. Such concurrent listening and speaking is known as 'shadowing', and has a strong reputation for being attention-demanding. Kleiman found that shadowing produced only moderate interference with judgements about the meanings of individual words when they were presented in pairs, whereas rhyming judgements were impaired. In another experiment reported in the same article, Kleiman observed the interference effects in a slightly different word-processing task. Instead of responding to a pair of words, readers were asked to look for specific relationships between a single word and a sentence. Four different sets of stimuli were used. The first condition used a visual-judgement task in which subjects had to say whether a word such as 'bury' looked like any of the words in the following sentence:

Yesterday the grand jury adjourned.

The second set of stimuli were used in a rhyming task in which the target word was matched against the sounds of words in the sentence. In the category judgement task, they had to say whether the word 'games' had any category members in

Everyone at home played monopoly.

In the fourth condition they were asked to judge whether a sentence made any sense. Both the visual-judgement and category-judgement tasks could be performed quite easily when the readers were distracted by the shadowing task. When they were asked to make a rhyming judgement, the shadowing interfered with performance, as it did with the judgements about rhyming word pairs. This is presumably because the task requires the same cognitive processors as shadowing – both tasks are speech-based.

The most interesting effect in Kleiman's experiments emerged when the shadowers were asked whether a sentence such as

Pizzas have been eating Jerry

made any sense. Performance again deteriorated, even though the category-judgement task had demonstrated that words in sentences could be processed despite distraction. We can conclude from Kleiman's experiments that when our attention is divided we can recognise the meanings of individual words adequately, but that they can be combined only with difficulty. Each of the words in the sentence will be recognised, but they are not easily integrated into an underlying meaning. Kleiman suggested that this was because his shadowing task had occupied space in the readers' 'working memory' – a kind of short-term memory useful in retaining numbers and words for just a few seconds. Unless we attend to the words which have been placed into working memory, they will not be retained. Retention alone is not sufficient for comprehension, but without this mental black-board it will be difficult to relate the meaning of one word to the meaning of another seen a few seconds later. Although we have concluded that the phonological processing of words is not necessary for their recognition, the conversion of print into a sound-based code does aid the comprehension of sentences. The advantage of using a sound-based code with working memory is that it produces memories which are more durable than those based upon a purely visual code, and this gives us more time to calculate the meaning of the sentence. Comprehension depends upon rapid word recognition, for if the reader is devoting time and attention to the individual words, then the relationships between words will not be appreciated and the integration of word meanings will not be calculated.

Conclusion: the importance of skilled word recognition

Finally, and by way of summarising and emphasising the main points of this chapter, an investigation by Graesser, Hoffman and Clark (1980) will be described briefly. A series of passages were read by adults in this experiment, with the time to read each sentence being measured. The adults were later divided into the faster 50 per cent of readers and the slower 50 per cent, and the influence of different passage features upon the reading times of the two groups was then calculated. Each sentence was classified according to a number of textual features which might increase the amount of time required to read it. The performances of the two groups of readers were then compared as a function of the features which might be predicted to increase the difficulty of the sentences.

On looking at the effectiveness of the various textual features, only small differences emerged between the two groups on a number of them, with the fast and slow readers being similarly affected by the unfamiliarity of the material in the passage and by the appearance of nouns not previously encountered in the text, and showing similar sensitivity to the distinction between narrative stories and non-fictional descriptive passages. The greatest differences between the groups were in understanding the different ideas (propositions) in a sentence, in dealing with problems of grammatical unpredictability, and most simply of all, in recognising words. As each of these features increased in complexity – more propositions, more unpredictability, more words in the sentence – so the faster readers increased their superiority over the slower readers. The feature of most interest is sentence length, because when we estimate the contribution made by each feature to the total amount of time spent reading, it is the number of words in a sentence which makes the largest difference between the two groups. The fast readers were more efficient than the slow readers in using grammatical predictability and in integrating different ideas in a sentence, but the factor accounting for the largest difference involved word-recognition processes. Words were recognised almost twice as quickly by the fast readers and, given the number of words in each sentence, this leads to a large efficiency difference between individuals.

The main conclusion to be drawn here is that the way to aid slow readers is to improve their word-recognition skills. A large sight vocabulary, acquired through practice, can aid rapid word recognition and leave the reader's attention free to consider the meaning of the sentence. When the reader does not need to dwell upon decoding, then words encountered early in a sentence will not have been forgotten and will, therefore, be available for integration with the words at the end of the sentence.

Acknowledgements

We are especially grateful to S.A. Clews and M. Wiser for their extensive comments on an early draft of this chapter. The Medical Research Council (project grant G8127736N) and the Science and Engineering Research Council (project grant GRCO2259) provided support during its preparation.

References

Baron, J. and Strawson, C. (1976) 'Use of orthographic and word-specific knowledge in reading words aloud', *Journal of Experimental Psychology: Human Perception and Performance*, 2, 386-93.
Barron, R.W. (1978) 'Reading skill and phonological coding in lexical access', in Gruneberg, M.M., Morris, P.E. and Sykes, R.N. (eds), *Practical Aspects of Memory*. Academic Press.
Barron, R.W. and Baron, J. (1977) 'How children get meaning from printed words', *Child Development*, 48, 587-94.

Briggs, P. and Underwood, G. (1982) 'Phonological coding in good and poor readers', *Journal of Experimental Child Psychology, 34,* 93-112.

Camp, B.W. and Dolcourt, J.L. (1977) 'Reading and spelling in good and poor readers', *Journal of Learning Disabilities, 10,* 300-7.

Frith, U. (1979) 'Reading by eye and writing by ear', in Kolers, P.A., Wrolstad, M.E. and Bouma, H. (eds), *Processing of Visible Language,* vol. 1. Plenum Press.

Frith, U. (1980) 'Unexpected spelling problems', in Frith, U. (ed.), *Cognitive Processes in Spelling.* Academic Press.

Glushko, R. (1979) 'The organization and activation of orthographic knowledge in reading aloud', *Journal of Experimental Psychology: Human Perception and Performance, 5,* 674-91.

Goodman, K.S. (1976) 'Reading: a psycholinguistic guessing game', in Singer, H. and Ruddell, R. (eds), *Theoretical Models and Processes of Reading,* 2nd edn. International Reading Association (IRA).

Graesser, A.C., Hoffman, N.L. and Clark, L.F. (1980) 'Structural components of reading time', *Journal of Verbal Learning and Verbal Behavior, 19,* 135-51.

Jastrzembski, J.E. (1981) 'Multiple meanings, number of related meanings, frequency of occurrence, and the lexicon', *Cognitive Psychology, 13,* 278-305.

Kay, J. and Marcel, A. (1981) 'One process, not two, in reading aloud: lexical analogies do the work of non-lexical rules', *Quarterly Journal of Experimental Psychology, 33A,* 397-413.

Kleiman, G.M. (1975) 'Speech recoding in reading', *Journal of Verbal Learning and Verbal Behavior, 14,* 323-39.

Mason, M. (1978) 'From print to sound in mature readers as a function of reader ability and two forms of orthographic regularity', *Memory and Cognition, 6,* 568-81.

Morton, J. (1969) 'Interaction of information in word recognition', *Psychological Review, 76,* 165-78.

Morton, J. (1980) 'The logogen model and orthographic structure', in Frith, U. (Ed.), *Cognitive Processes in Spelling.* Academic Press.

O'Regan, K. (1979) 'Saccade size in reading: evidence for the linguistic control hypothesis', *Perception and Psychophysics, 25,* 501-9.

Perin, D. (1983) 'Phonemic segmentation and spelling', *British Journal of Psychology, 74,* 129-44.

Smith, F. (1978) *Understanding Reading.* Holt, Rinehart & Winston.

Stanovich, K.E., West, R.F. and Feeman, D.J. (1981) 'A longitudinal study of sentence context effects in second-grade children: Tests of an interactive-compensatory model', *Journal of Experimental Child Psychology, 32,* 185-99.

Underwood, G. (1982) 'Attention and awareness in cognitive and motor

C

skills', in Underwood, G. (ed.), *Aspects of Consciousness*, Vol. 3. Academic Press.

Underwood, G. and Bargh, K. (1982) 'Word shape, orthographic regularity, and contextual interactions in a reading task', *Cognition, 12*, 197-209.

Underwood, G. and Briggs, P. (1984) 'The development of word recognition processes', *British Journal of Psychology, 75*, 243-55.

Underwood, G., Whitfield, A. and Winfield, J. (1982) 'Effects of contextual constraints and non-fixated words in a simple reading task', *Journal of Research in Reading, 5*, 89-99.

West, R.F. and Stanovich, K.E. (1978) 'Automatic contextual facilitation in readers of three ages', *Child Development, 49*, 717-27.

4

New directions in text research and readability

Colin Harrison

The background

Anyone who has an historical interest in the topic of readability will be familiar with its dramatic vacillations in popularity. More than once in the past 50 years the concept of readability measurement and prediction has been castigated as facile and simplistic, despite the earnest attempts of most readability researchers themselves to portray their work in a balanced and untendentious way. Kintsch and Vipond (1979) have discussed some of these changes in popularity, and have offered an interesting explanation for the question they ask (and answer) themselves: 'Who cares about readability? Psychologists don't – not any more.'

The analysis offered by Kintsch and Vipond essentially argues that research on readability has been thoroughly practical, but hopelessly unanalytical. Conversely, psychology itself has been in no shape to deliver the goods it promised: if educationists were atheoretical, psychologists for their part were producing theories which were too crude to be of much use to educational researchers. This was especially true in the areas of information processing which were of special interest to them. What Kintsch and Vipond argue is that readability research has asserted an interest in helping to produce a sensitive matching of reader to printed text, but has in fact ignored one of the most vital aspects of this – the question of text-reader interaction. This weakness has been largely due, they suggest, to the fact that readability research has been based on an impoverished psychology of reading. They sum up their view of the current state of research using predictive readability formulae in the following way: 'Formulas do a job, but they leave a lot unexplained.'

In this chapter we shall go deeper into the question of how limited that job is, and shall look at the results of some current formula-based work. More importantly, we shall also consider some of the most recent approaches that psychologists have adopted in their attempts to bridge the gap which has hitherto existed between psychological theory and educational practice. There are many signs that although the new tools for analysis are not simple ones, they are offering exciting insights into the problems of matching readers to texts, and helping to produce a deeper response and more effective learning.

What can readability formulae do?

Predictive readability formulae such as those of Flesch (1948) and Dale and Chall (1948) have been widely used on both sides of the Atlantic for decades. They are just two of 50 or so formulae, charts and graphs available to teachers who wish to assess the difficulty of prose objectively (see Harrison, 1980, for a review). In a useful comparative study, Entin and Klare (1978) used the statistical technique of factor analysis to compare the results of a number of independently conducted studies of readability. Their conclusion was that despite the large number of variables considered by the studies, the traditional variables of word difficulty and sentence difficulty were by far the most important. Two additional factors, idea density and word diversity, accounted for a small but noteworthy proportion of difficulty.

As an example of the continuing usefulness of the

traditional approach, we can consider the fascinating cross-cultural work of Bjornsson (1983). Early in the 1960s, Bjornsson constructed a readabiity formula on the simplest possible lines: sentence length + word length = lix. Sentence length is the number of words per sentence, word length Bjornsson defines as the percentage of words with more than six letters, and lix is simply an abbreviation of the Swedish word for readability index. The formula was tried out on thousands of texts, and norms established using pooled subjective judgements as the initial criterion for fixing and comparing difficulty levels.

Bjornsson's approach differed from that of many earlier researchers in two important ways: first, he set out at an early stage to make his formula one which would be useful for making cross-cultural comparisons, and second, he chose not to use the statistical technique of multiple regression. For the cross-cultural comparisons separate investigations were conducted for Swedish, Danish, English, French, German and Finnish. In these studies, Bjornsson used groups of 24 or more readers (of whom half at least would have been native speakers) and calculated correlations to check the reliability of their judgements. On sets of 100 texts, the correlations were on average 0.99, which suggests that for adults at least, there is a high level of agreement about what is difficult. One point to mention is that Bjornsson avoided using raters who knew anything about readability research – he wanted overall difficulty, not linguistic variables as such, to be the criterion used by the readers. From each country's findings, Bjornsson derived a lix score which seemed to represent 'normal difficulty' from a range of material including children's books, factual prose (written for non-specialists) and technical literature. The final lix scores varied: Swedish was 39, English 40, German 45 and French 46. Finnish had fewer words per sentence on average, but had 48 per cent of words with six or more letters, 19 per cent more than German, which was the next highest. This gave Finnish a very high lix score of 60.

It is worth spending a moment considering what might seem a very technical matter, but it is one with important practical implications. Bjornsson decided not to use a formula derived from multiple regression analysis. In doing so he departed from the precedent set by many of the best known formula constructors, including Flesch and Dale. Why was this? Bjornsson explains in a way which serves to remind us that the mathematical precision of a readability formula may be misleading. Despite all his careful preliminary research, Bjornsson discovered that if he calculated a formula from one half of his data he obtained a completely different equation from that which was obtained from the other half. Furthermore, when he checked back on the correlation between his simple lix values and the criterion of pooled estimates of difficulty, he found that the figure was 0.92, which was exactly the same as that obtained from the multiple regression. In other words, the regression formula approach added nothing. He decided, therefore, that he would not use it, and gained a great deal in time saved in calculation without losing anything in validity.

Bjornsson went on to study the newspapers of 11 countries, and found substantial differences, which he argued could not be attributed to the idiosyncrasies of the languages. To begin with, he noticed a number of interesting trends within Sweden itself. National newspapers were more difficult than local ones, and morning papers were more difficult than those sold in the evening. There had been a staggering decrease in difficulty over a century in the largest Swedish daily, *Dagens Nyheter*, which roughly corresponded to the difference between children's books and adult literature.

English has about the same lix level as the Nordic languages and this enabled Bjornsson to compare Scandinavian newspapers with those from English-speaking countries. London's evening paper was similar in lix score to a Swedish evening paper, but there were major differences in word and sentence scores. Swedish papers had longer words, while the English paper had about five words per sentence more. In the case of the morning papers, it seems that papers such as *The Times* and the *Daily Telegraph* are much more difficult than their Swedish counterparts. Indeed, if the scores are in reality comparable across countries, *The Times* today is about as difficult as *Dagens Nyheter* was in 1900! This situation appears to be even worse as we move south through Europe, since even allowing for differences between the languages, Bjornsson notes that Italian, Spanish and Portuguese papers have very high scores, due in large part to sentences with a mean length of over 30 words. He finds it hard to resist the conclusion that there are some very important implications here, which extend beyond the domain of reading research and education, and touch upon the fundamental issues of democracy and equality.

Bjornsson's research is thorough, interesting and reported with due emphasis on its areas of possible weakness or unreliability. It will be equally interesting to see more work done extending his methods to the texts used in schools. If this is to happen, however, it will be necessary for those who do the work to pay heed to other researchers who have pointed out a major flaw in much readability research. This flaw relates to the difficult problem of sampling.

The problem of sampling in readability measurement

Readability researchers often emphasise that it is not possible to use a formula to assess difficulty at the individual sentence level; a formula or graph can only make predictions about difficulty at a global level. But the question remains, how confident can we be that a formula score is truly representative of the overall difficulty level? Stokes (1978) studied history books and found wide variation between 100-word samples of text. These variations were so great that he questioned the applicability of formulae which used this approach to sampling.

More recently, Fitzgerald (1981) gave a whole catalogue of problems associated with sampling. She used a range of textbooks and workbooks (but analysed large segments of text only – not short sections such as questions or exercises). Following the method proposed by Fry (1977), she used readability scores based on groups of three 100-word passages, and found disturbing differences. In one study, based on an analysis of five high-school textbooks, Fitzgerald took six sets of three samples from each book, and found that individual samples spanned a range of at least ten grades within each book, and the means of the sets of three had on average a range of three grades within each book.

The working assumption behind the Fry graph is that the mean obtained from three samples approximates to the population mean (i.e. the actual difficulty of the book). This was far from the case. Fitzgerald calculated the critical number of samples needed to be 80 per cent certain that the mean score would be no more than one year out, and found that in one book it was 72 samples – which amounted to nearly half the book! The obvious solution, one might think, would be to increase the number of 100-word samples taken, to six or perhaps nine, but this too would be of little value if there were great variability within the book. Fitzgerald found that for some books, an increase to six or even nine samples actually produced means which systematically departed even further from the population mean – the true overall difficulty level. Only after the number of samples taken approached or exceeded the critical number did the mean of the samples agree with the population mean. Even then there were some books for which not even the critical number was enough, and nothing less than the whole text had to be sampled to determine its average readability.

Do we now hear yet another death knell for readability studies? Not necessarily, since both teachers and researchers will ultimately use readability formulae for just so long as they find them of some value. Fitzgerald herself does not go so far as to suggest that they should not be used at all. Rather, she urges both researchers and publishers to use readability estimates with extreme caution, and where possible, to work from population means rather than inadequate samples.

Current advances in new technology mean that computer analysis of complete texts is already possible. Most books will soon be set completely by computer, and thus the publisher will have a machine-readable version available for analysis. It might otherwise cost a good deal of money to do this. In the future, therefore, we must encourage publishers to be a little more forthcoming about the basis on which they offer readability data, and look carefully to see whether what they have calculated really is the population mean of the book in question.

From the teacher's point of view, another implication arises from the study by Fitzgerald. This is the distinction between local and global readability means. As Fitzgerald pointed out, the variability between books is tremendous: some books are fairly stable, but others vary enormously from section to section. If this is the case, would it not be preferable in certain instances to consider local readability as the population mean which interests us? If a book contains a number of chapters or sections, which may even have been written by different authors, of what value to us is the global population mean based on the average over all chapters? If we are wanting to consider the relationship between readability and comprehension for one particular topic or passage, then it would almost certainly be preferable to consider the local readability of that chapter or section. The issue of sampling adequacy does not arise if our analysis is based on the whole of the text under consideration. Fitzgerald's warnings apply to the difficulties of generalising about global readability from a small number of samples of an extensive text. If we apply the concept of local readability, then these problems are by-passed. The question which remains is that of minimum sample size and, in general, other researchers have tended to avoid applying formulae to texts of less than 150 words in length.

Is cloze procedure an appropriate measure of comprehension?

In the 1960s, cloze procedure came to be seen by some researchers as the answer to many of the problems of validly measuring text difficulty. Bormuth's landmark study (1969) seemed to offer the promise not only of more valid formulae which would incorporate the results of new insights in linguistics, but also a means of readily assessing whether a person was understanding a text or not. The mean percentage correct cloze score (i.e., the percentage of deleted words correctly replaced by the reader) appeared to give an indication of how well a passage was understood. Thus, a cloze score of 60 per cent would indicate fairly full comprehension, 45 per cent would suggest some problems, while 35 per cent would suggest that a reader was at his or her frustration level.

Recently, however, this view has been called into question. Despite the finding of fairly high correlations between cloze and reading comprehension as measured by multiple-choice tests (in the order of 0.6 and above, depending on the nature of the study), some experiments have suggested that cloze may be measuring what one might call potential for understanding, rather than comprehension itself.

Bailey and Harrison (1984) followed up the research of Cohen (1975), which had reported that percentage cloze scores seemed to represent different levels of understanding according to the nature of the subject. Cohen had found that materials at similar readability levels as measured by a formula produced very different cloze test scores: 30 per cent for literature, 37 per cent for science, and 40 per cent for social studies. Bailey and Harrison found that for certain types of passage cloze scores were potentially unreliable indicators of comprehension. In a cloze test on a difficult science text, for example, a phrase such as 'pulmonary artery' or 'nervous stimulation' may occur a number of times. Once a reader has seen the phrase, and comes across '___ artery' or 'nervous ___', it may be possible to insert the correct answer without having much idea what the word actually means. If this occurred a number of times, an artificially high cloze score would be the result. By contrast, in a literary passage, especially when using verbatim scoring (see Harrison, 1980, for a discussion of different cloze scoring methods), a cloze score may misrepresent understanding by being artificially low. A reader can be fully understanding a section from a story, and yet fail to insert the exact word in a phrase such as 'watched the fleeting panorama of ___ shop fronts', when no other information about the shop fronts is given. In these two examples, we are reminded that what cloze is measuring is the predictability, or more accurately, the redundancy within a passage, and this may or may not be closely related to its comprehensibility.

Another way of asking whether cloze gets close to measuring comprehension is to consider what would happen if the sentences in a passage were randomly re-ordered. As we shall see in the later sections of this chapter, contemporary theories of comprehension give great weight to the way in which information is integrated between sentences. If cloze is a sensitive measure of this aspect of comprehension, we would expect readers to do very poorly if they were presented with a cloze test on a passage in which all the sentences had been mixed up. In fact, this does not tend to happen.

Shanahan, Kamil and Tobin (1982) reported a very interesting study in which they not only examined the effect of normal and scrambled passages on cloze test scores, but also compared the results against tests of recall for the same passage presented without deletions. The cloze scores for the two conditions, normal and scrambled, hardly differed at all (49 per cent for the normal; 46 per cent for the scrambled), which suggested that the re-ordering did not have much effect. However, the recall scores told a different story. Percentage recall scores went like this:

Intact/normal passage 31
Intact/scrambled 24
Cloze/normal passage 20
Cloze/scrambled 13

These results indicated significantly lower recall scores for the scrambled version, whether a reader was working from the version with no words missed out or doing a cloze test. The cloze scores alone did not suggest this, however, and one is bound to ponder the significance of this. If cloze only measures comprehension at the phrase or sentence level, it has severe limitations. Even if it measures the use of redundancy up to ten words either side of the deletion, this is still not the same as measuring comprehension: as we saw in the Bailey and Harrison study, redundancy and comprehensibility can be very different aspects of a text.

Cloze procedure is a very useful tool. It was first used in readability experiments (Taylor, 1953), but has subsequently been used for formal and informal testing of reading comprehension, and in a dozen different ways for work in reading development. It will be interesting to see the extent to which cloze remains a key concept in future readability studies.

The need for a broader view of text difficulty

The past ten years have seen something of a revolution in text analysis, and in our understanding of how the results of such work might be applied in the classroom. In broad terms, the shifts of emphasis have been related to two central themes: first, that notions of reading comprehension must take greater account of what is going on in the mind of the reader, and second, that methods of text analysis must take greater account of what is going on beyond the sentence boundary. This dual emphasis on the reader and on analysis of texts in units larger than a sentence seems to offer the beginnings at least of a new approach to text research, one which moves beyond a correlational approach to readability and starts instead to identify causal relationships between aspects of texts and difficulties in comprehension.

To consider the importance of the role of the reader as an active partner in the process of comprehension, we can begin with the concept of *schemata*. Schema theories were first popularised by Bartlett in the 1920s and Piaget in the 1930s. They put forward the notion that we construct routine groupings of aspects of experience, *schemata*, which tend to occur regularly together. These schemata are stored away, and produced when appropriate. There are a number of types of schemata. We have schemata for action, for example: we do not have to replan how to get dressed every day; for many of us, the decision about what shoes to wear is quite enough of a problem for one morning. We also have schemata for comprehension. Consider the following brief passage:

> Mary heard the alarm and groaned inwardly, pulling the covers over her head. She tried to remember whether there was any milk in the icebox.

A reader could make a number of inferences about this passage:

> Mary is female, more probably an adult than a child;
> it is morning;
> Mary does not want to get up for some reason;
> Mary is in bed;
> she lives in a house with a refrigerator;
> the house is possibly in North America, and so on.

When one begins to list the dozens of schema-based inferences which even such a brief passage as this evokes, it soon becomes clear that there is much more to comprehension than vocabulary and sentence structure – comprehension is crucially dependent upon schemata. The richness and variety of the reader's own schemata, and the extent to which (in a particular case) the author and reader share a similar schema, will determine what is understood, what is inferred, and, to a great extent, what is learned.

In a classic experiment, Bransford and Johnson (1972) showed the vital importance not only of possessing prior knowledge, but of activating it, if learning is to take place. They tested the comprehension and recall of matched groups of subjects on a simple passage. The passage was all about washing clothes, but only one group was told this in advance. The second group was told the title after they had read the passage, while the third group were not told the title at all. The passage did not contain many clues to its overall theme. Instead, it contained sentences such as, 'First you arrange things into different groups. Of course, one pile may be sufficient depending on how much there is to do.' Not surprisingly, the group which had been told the topic in advance performed best on the tests. What is surprising is that the group which was told the topic immediately after the reading was not able to make any use of the information; they did just as poorly as the 'no topic' group.

What this study showed was the importance of activating the appropriate schemata. Each of the groups possessed the necessary prior knowledge, but only one group had that knowledge activated. There are clear implications here for teachers. The systematic activation of prior knowledge can act to prepare for and deepen the likely response to a text.

Langer (1982), in an admirable book which attempts to bridge the gap between researchers and teachers, explains how this can be done systematically. There is no space here for a full account of her system, but its key characteristics are phases of (a) free associations with the topic, (b) reflections on each other's associations, (c) collaborative reformulation of prior knowledge. During these phases, the teacher (and ultimately the student) assesses the level of prior knowledge, associations and responses. These may be at the level of *little*–associations, anecdotes, etc., *some*–examples, attributes, defining features, etc., or *more*–superordinate concepts, definitions, analogies, etc. Langer has done a good deal of research into the evaluation of this approach to schema activation, and she is convinced that it helps poor readers and good readers alike to learn more from difficult textbooks.

Readability beyond the sentence boundary

Not many years ago, it seemed that almost all readability research, and almost all research in linguistics confined itself to the analysis of units no larger than a sentence. This is no longer the case. In psychology, work clustered around the ideas of Frederiksen (1975), Meyer (1975), Rumelhart (1975), Kintsch (1977), Thorndyke (1977) and Mandler and Johnson (1977) has led to dozens of studies based on an analysis of various types of text structure and the relationship between text structure and recall. In linguistics, the seminal work of Grimes (1975), Halliday and Hasan (1976) and van Dijk (1977) has been equally fruitful in prompting new insights into how texts are bound together beyond the sentence. Some of these studies are extremely technical, but they have all producd other studies which have direct classroom relevance.

The general questions which all these researchers address are: how are texts built up, and how does their structure determine what a reader is able to comprehend and recall? Research work carried out in linguistics is generally more descriptive than practical in terms of classroom applications, but Chapman (1983) provides a useful account of the educational relevance of work in linguistics, giving special emphasis to the concept of cohesion in texts.

Of the studies done by psychologists, one might begin by referring to those conducted by Mandler and Johnson on what are called story grammars. How is it that we are able to predict the ending of a story (and even castigate an ending for being *too* predictable)? When we say that a child enjoys the security of a familiar story structure, what tools have we for analysing that structure? Why is it that we can all recall and retell a story, but find it hard to recall and retell the contents of a textbook or scientific paper? Mandler and Johnson (1977) suggest that a story grammar, in which elements (such as setting, event, episode, consequence and resolution) are combined according to a set of implicit rules, offers a mechanism for answering many of these questions.

This approach certainly does offer a basis for analysing texts which touches upon aspects of likely response that no traditional readability formula would measure. One problem, however, is that only a subset of all texts do in fact have what might loosely be called a story structure. Most textbooks are not written like a thriller, though it might be interesting if they were. (*The Double Helix*, by James Watson, which tells of the race to find the molecular structure of DNA, is perhaps an example of what such a book might be like.) Because of their limited applicability, story grammars might be too crude or too restricted in their potential application to be of value across the whole range of school subjects.

A different but related approach was that of Meyer (1975), who considered the knowledge structure of texts, and produced a type of grammar which would cope better with the variety of types of organisation and structure found in textbooks.

Meyer's analysis (see figure 4.1) produces in diagram form a representation of the information in a passage organised into a hierarchy, which would enable a teacher systematically to examine comprehension and the effects of different types of text manipulation. In the figure, the main information to be recalled is shown in block letters, while the logical relationships are shown in lower case letters at the nodes (joining points) of the lines.

```
  1   Response
  2   problem
  3   APPEAR TO BE

  4      patient
  5      PERSONS WITH AFFECTIVE DISORDERS

  6      latter
  7      OUT OF PHASE WITH NORMAL 24-HOUR DAY
  8      evidence
  9      ARE SHEDDING SOME LIGHT ON AFFECTIVE DISORDERS covariance, antecedent

 10         patient
 11         RESEARCH RESULTS

 12            evidence
 13            collection
 14            NOREPINEPHRINE AND SEROTONIN HAVE BEEN IMPLICATED IN DEPRESSION

 15               specific
 16               collection
 17               MEASURING THE HORMONE MELATONIN

 18                  specific
 19                  SEEMS TO RUN

 20                     patient
 21                     MELATONIN

 22                        attribution
 23                        AN INDICATOR OF NOREPINEPHRINE ACTIVITY

 24                        range
 25                        THROUGH A CYCLE

 26                           explanation
 27                           PEAKS IN JANUARY AND JULY AND HITS VALLEYS IN MAY AND OCTOBER

 28               (MEASURING) PLATELET SEROTONIN

 29                  specific
 30                  APPEARS TO BE ON A REVERSE CYCLE

 31      ARE

 32         patient
 33         DAILY BIOLOGICAL RHYTHMS

 34            attribution
 35            OF SOME PERSONS WITH AFFECTIVE DISORDERS

 36-           latter
 37            SLIGHTLY OUT OF PHASE WITH THE STANDARD 24-HOUR DAY

 38            explanation
 39            WOULD GO TO BED AND WAKE UP SOMEWHAT EARLIER THAN USUAL

 40               setting time
 41               SEVERAL DAYS BEFORE THE PERIODIC MANIC PHASE SETS IN

 42   covariance, consequent
 43   MAY BE

 44      force
 45      SLIGHTLY ABNORMAL BIOLOGICAL RHYTHM

 46      patient
 47      KEY FACTORS IN THE DEVELOPMENT OF DEPRESSION AND MANIC DEPRESSION

 48   solution
 49   CHANGING SLEEP-WAKE FACTORS CAN TRIGGER DRAMATIC IMPROVEMENTS

 50      explanation
 51      REASONED

 52         agent
 53         INVESTIGATORS

 54         WAS ASSOCIATED WITH covariance, antecedent

 55            force
 56            SLEEP-WAKE CHANGE

 57            patient
 58            SHIFT AWAY FROM DEPRESSION

 59         MANIPULATING covariance, consequent

 60            manner
 61            INTENTIONALLY

 62            patient
 63            (SLEEP-WAKE) PATTERN

 64            benefactive
 65            DEPRESSIVES
```

Figure 4.1 The content structure of 'Cracking the Cycles of Depression and Mania'

Source: B.J.F. Meyer, *The Organisation of Prose and its Effect on Recall* (North Holland, 1975)

The way in which the logical structure of a passage is perceived by different readers can differ enormously. Just as some readers may not share an action or background knowledge schema with an author, so they may not have ready access to a logic schema which would help them to use the passage effectively. In a celebrated piece of research, Marshall and Glock (1978-9) examined this phenomenon, and the results of the study have important implications for teachers.

What Marshall and Glock did was to vary certain aspects of text structure, and look at the effect in terms of how well subjects were able to write about what they recalled from the passage in question. They looked at such things as whether *if-then* relationships between clauses were present or absent, and also changed the order of several sentences. It was hoped that by noting the differences and similarities between the passage read and what was recalled, the authors would be able to draw inferences about how information is organised in memory.

In the event, their most important findings were not ones which had been anticipated at the planning stage of the study. The 160 adult subjects who took part in the study represented a range of reading abilities. This would be a natural aim for any researcher to achieve, and in order to obtain a full range of reading ability Marshall and Glock recruited one population from a community college, and another from undergraduates at Cornell University. During the scoring of the recall tests, it was noticed that those of the Cornell students seemed much more full than those of the community college students, and the researchers decided to analyse the two sets of results separately, instead of together, as had originally been planned.

What was discovered was that, in general, the researchers could manipulate the passages in all kinds of ways without the Cornell students being thrown: *if-then* relations could be missed out, the logical structure of the passage could be masked by inserting a crucial sentence in the wrong place; yet the Cornell students still performed well on the recall tests. By contrast, the community college students recalled more information when the *if-then* relations were stated explicitly than they did when they were implicit only. Equally, the community college students recalled more information when the relative importance of different ideas was made more explicit.

What Marshall and Glock concluded was that the community college students responded to the surface structure of the discourse only, while the Cornell students responded to its semantic and logical structure. It was as if the Cornell students were capable of ignoring surface structure, and could refer to the passage's deep structure as if it were complete. They could infer the complete message even when it was not explicitly stated in the text.

What conclusions should we draw from this study? First, we must note that the researchers found that, for a start, the Cornell students had greater prior knowledge of both the passages studied in the experiment than the community college students. This reminds us that the pre-reading activities advocated by Langer, to which we referred above, will be especially useful for less fluent readers. If prior knowledge is low, then it is all the more vital to activate and organise it.

Another conclusion must be that if we as teachers are relative experts in our own subjects, and tend to read textbooks in our own subject area with the same skills as the Cornell students, then we may be insensitive to inadequacies in those textbooks. The Cornell students, you will recall, ignored missing causal links and coped happily with missing information on main points and even corrupted sentence ordering. If this is what fluent readers do, then there is surely a sense in which an expert is a slightly unreliable judge of how clearly a book is written. The expert can judge the content, but the views of a novice may well be valuable in helping to judge the effectiveness of how that content is put over.

This final point was illustrated in an experiment (Gordon,

1983) in which two classes of children aged 12 were asked to identify what they thought were the difficult parts of passages from a history textbook. They then worked as a class to produce a new rewritten version which they hoped would be more comprehensible. In a crossover design, each class did comprehension tests on four passages – two original ones, and two which had been rewritten by the other group. What Gordon found was that the passages rewritten by the class containing the most poor readers were the ones which were subsequently found to be the most comprehensible. In other words, children who were poor readers seemed to have greater insight into likely difficulties for other readers.

It is worth noting that although the children produced passages which facilitated greater learning, the changes which they made were not necessarily ones which would be picked up by a readability formula. The children did make changes in vocabulary, substituting 'changed' for 'alternated' for example, and they also changed syntax, preferring a main clause, 'When the wool had been cleaned and combed' to 'The raw wool having been cleaned and combed'. But perhaps the most crucial changes they made were to what Gordon referred to as the 'macrostructure signalling' within the passage. Instead of the simple phrase 'Hand cards were like' the group preferred 'Hand cards, *on the other hand*, were like'. Instead of 'It has been thoroughly cleaned, . . . It has also been carded or combed' they preferred '*Firstly*, it has been cleaned, . . . *Secondly*, it has been carded or combed'.

These changes introduced by 12 year-old children are precisely the type of text feature which Marshall and Glock found to be essential if poor readers were to learn all they could from a passage. What Gordon found was that, given the context of a mutually supportive group-writing task, poor readers themselves were able to do the job of constructing the missing macrostructure of a text, and thus could overcome some of its difficulties. His findings remind us again that text difficulty is not a purely static thing – it is the result of the meeting of a reader and a text, and a measure of the extent to which the linguistic and experiential worlds of the reader and author coincide, or fail to coincide.

In the next ten years we shall be fortunate if we witness as productive a period for text research as that which has just ended. Readability, as we have known it, may not be dead, but the utility of formulae must continue to be seriously questioned in the light of current research findings. At the same time, researchers will no doubt continue to be inventive in harnessing the insights of teachers and the tools of linguistic analysis in the quest for more sensitive measures of text difficulty. In Austria, for example, Bamberger (personal communication) is working with teachers on a 35 point readability check-list which attempts to encompass many of the 'new' variables referred to earlier in this chapter, such as cohesion, macrostructure signalling and prior knowledge. If past experience is a reliable guide, there will be no shortage of similarly bold attempts to transform the findings of workers in linguistics and psychology into classroom action, and to ensure that the concept of readability remains a useful one.

References

Bailey, M.C. and Harrison, C. (1984) 'Cloze procedure as a measure of reading comprehension: the effects of variations in subject matter on textual redundancy', *Human Learning, 3*, 185-201.

Bjornsson, C.H. (1983) 'Readability of newspapers in 11 languages', *Reading Research Quarterly, 18*, 480-97.

Bormuth, J.R. (1969) *Development of Readability Analyses.* Final Report, Project No. 7-0052. Bureau of Research, United States Office of Education (USOE).

Bransford, J.D. and Johnson, M.K. (1972) 'Consideration of some problems of comprehension', *Journal of Verbal Learning and Verbal Behavior, 11*, 717-26.

Chapman, L.J. (1983) *Reading Development and Cohesion.* Longman.

Cohen, J.H. (1975) 'The effect of content area material on cloze test performance', *Journal of Reading, 19*, 247-50.

Dale, E. and Chall, J.S. (1948) 'A formula for predicting readability', *Educational Research Bulletin, 27*, 11-20; 37-54.

Entin, E.B. and Klare, G.R. (1978) 'Factor analyses of three correlation matrices of readability variables', *Journal of Reading Behaviour, 10,* 279-90.

Fitzgerald, G.G. (1981) 'How many samples give a good readability estimate? – the Fry graph', *Journal of Reading, 24,* 404-10.

Flesch, R.F. (1948) 'A new readability yardstick', *Journal of Applied Psychology, 32,* 221-33.

Fredericksen, C.H. (1975) 'Representing logical and semantic structure of knowledge acquired from discourse', *Cognitive Psychology, 7,* 371-458.

Fry, E. (1977) 'Fry's readability graph: clarifications, validity and extension to level 17', *Journal of Reading, 21,* 242-52.

Gordon, A. (1983) 'A study of the effects of peer group rewriting of history text on children's comprehension of difficult material'. MEd. dissertation, Nottingham University.

Grimes, J.E. (1975) *The Thread of Discourse.* Mouton.

Halliday, M.A.K. and Hasan, R. (1976) *Cohesion in English.* Longman.

Harrison, C. (1980) *Readability in the Classroom.* Cambridge University Press.

Kintsch, W. (1977) 'On comprehending stories', in Just, M.A. and Carpenter, P.A. (eds), *Cognitive Processes in Comprehension.* Erlbaum.

Kintsch, W. and Vipond, D. (1977) 'Reading comprehension and readability in educational practice and psychological theory', in Nilsson, L.-G. (ed.), *Perspectives on Memory Research.* Erlbaum.

Langer, J.A. (1982) 'Facilitating text processing: the elaboration of prior knowledge', in Langer, J.A. and Smith-Burke, M.T. (eds), *Reader Meets Author: Bridging the Gap.* IRA.

Mandler, J.M. and Johnson, N.S. (1977) 'Remembrance of things parsed: story structure and recall', *Cognitive Psychology, 9,* 111-51.

Marshall, N. and Glock, M.D. (1978-9) 'Comprehension of connected discourse: a study into the relationship between the structure of text and information recalled', *Reading Research Quarterly, 14,* 10-56.

Meyer, B.J.F. (1975) *The Organisation of Prose and its Effect on Recall.* North Holland.

Rumelhart, D.E. (1975) 'Notes on a schema for stories', in Bobrow, D.G. and Collins, A.M. (eds), *Representation and Understanding: Studies in Cognitive Science.* Academic Press.

Shanahan, T., Kamil, M.L. and Tobin, A.W. (1982) 'Cloze as a measure of intersentential comprehension', *Reading Research Quarterly, 17,* 229-55.

Stokes, A. (1978) 'The reliability of readability formulae', *Journal of Research in Reading, 1,* 21-34.

Taylor, W.L. (1953) 'Cloze procedure: a new tool for measuring readability', *Journalism Quarterly, 30,* 415-33.

Thorndyke, P.W. (1977) 'Cognitive structures in comprehension and memory of narrative discourse', *Cognitive Psychology, 9,* 77-110.

van Dijk, T.A. (1977) 'Semantic macrostructures and knowledge frames in discourse comprehension', in Just, M.A. and Carpenter, P.A. (eds), *Cognitive Processes in Comprehension*. Erlbaum.

5

Children as writers

John Harris

Retrospect

It may not be too extreme to suggest that the last few years have seen a quiet revolution in the direction taken by our thinking about writing development and the teaching of writing in schools. Whether this redirection has yet had much effect in the classroom is another matter entirely – from my own observations there seems as yet to have been few major changes in practice. Nevertheless, in the course of a great deal of inservice work with both primary and secondary teachers I have gained the impression that many are dissatisfied with current practice without knowing with any certainty how to improve matters.

The exciting and liberating redirection achieved during the sixties, usually characterised as the creative writing movement, has lost its way. The products often disappoint: the criteria for evaluation both of product and of teaching are hard to determine. This is because there is a fundamental tension involved. If you expect a child to write about a personal experience, engagement with that experience has to be regarded as a priority. Nevertheless, the writing remains as something separate from the experience and if teachers do not know how they can usefully respond to the writing as a text, then their part in helping children improve their writing is insignificant.

The creative writing movement has also perpetuated a polarity, particularly in the primary curriculum, between the creative and the rest of the written work undertaken. There has never been any certainty as to how this other writing can be classified, whether as 'factual', 'non-creative', 'project' or 'topic' writing. The confusion over nomenclature betrays a deeper confusion over aims in relation to writing. The Bullock report (DES, 1975) found that a significant proportion of the writing in primary schools that could not be characterised as 'creative writing' was copied from source materials such as reference books. The primary survey (DES, 1978) corroborated this finding. Yet both Bullock and the more recent Oracle project (Galton, Simon and Kroll, 1980) point to the dominant place of writing in the school day, despite differences in the detailed findings which can be accounted for by different observational methodologies. Nor should we think that the situation is better at secondary level. Again a recent HMI survey (DES, 1979) supports the salutary comment of Britton that 'much writing at Secondary level lacks any real sense of purpose.' (See Britton et al., 1975.)

In the post-Bullock years, thinking about writing at secondary level in particular has been dominated by the model developed by Britton and his colleagues at the London Institute for the Schools Council. While I believe that this work has promoted a great deal of useful thinking about the place and function of writing in the curriculum, I am not alone in doubting the validity of the model. Whitehead (1978) and Williams (1977) have both offered perceptive critiques which suggest that, at the very least, Britton's notion of writing modes – the expressive, poetic and transactional – and his categories of audience should not be regarded as unproblematic.

Although this is not an appropriate context in which to offer a discussion of Britton's theories, as I develop my argument about a redirection in writing some specific criticisms of the work will emerge. Above all, it is worth bearing in mind that Britton's work has little to say directly about writing development. What it does say is neatly summed up by Bereiter (1980): 'the disappointing message of the Schools' Council research is that as soon as we begin to look beyond syntax, vocabulary and the like and try to investigate functional aspects of student writing, we begin to find out more about the school system than we find out about children.'

Bereiter's mention of syntax provides a timely cue for looking at another area of research into writing development which, it was hoped, would give us clear indicators of development through the years of schooling. The basic procedure was to identify selected features, such as the length of sentences or the incidence of subordination, and to see whether these provided a measure of maturation in writing. Out of this type of work a broad area of agreement has emerged, as a brief review will show.

An early researcher, La Brant (1933), worked at clause level, distinguishing independent and dependent (subordinate) clauses and classifying dependent clauses as noun, adjectival and adverbial. Adverbial clauses she subdivided according to functional relationship (time and causal, for instance) – the categories will be familiar to anyone nurtured in the traditional approach to clause analysis! La Brant established a range of general findings not seriously challenged since; namely, that development in writing was evidenced by an increase in the proportion of dependent to independent clauses, by the gross length of the writing (the number of words), by an increase in average length of sentence and by a growing complexity of sentence structure. Although this last point is not in broad terms contentious, it should be noted that La Brant did not clearly establish criteria for judging complexity. One of the problems that arises with this approach is the validity of the features isolated. A relative clause counts as dependent whereas an adjective modifying a noun clearly does not. Yet if we look at the procedures for embedding, it is not easy to see why one should count and the other not. Consider the sentence:

Roger has a black dog called Ben.

This can be thought of as comprising the following clauses:

Roger has a dog
The dog is black
It is called Ben

These can be combined in various ways which would 'score' in a count of dependent clauses, e.g.:

Roger has a dog, Ben, who is black,
Roger has a black dog, who is called Ben,

while the initial version does not. Who is to say that the first is not as 'complex' as the second or third? If we use 'complex' in a technical sense where it is opposed to 'simplex' then the judgement is sound. Otherwise, it is not.

Hunt (1965) refined the method of analysis by proposing four units for quantification. Apart from the word, the clause and the sentence (orthographically signalled), he used what he termed the 'T-Unit'. This he describes as 'a minimal terminable unit, consisting of one main clause plus any subordinate clause or non-clausal structure (such as a phrase) that is attached to or embedded in it'. He used this classification to analyse the writing of 9, 13 and 17 year olds. His general findings are in accord with those of La Brant, but more refined. He found that there was an increase with age in the number of words per clause, clauses per T-unit and words per T-unit. Equally, with age, there were fewer T-units per sentence (fewer co-ordinated clauses, for example), fewer but longer single clause T-units and, as a corollary, more multi-clause T-units. He found also that the incidence of relative clauses was a very clear indicator of development, increasing four times from the youngest group of writers in his sample to the eldest.

Loban (1963 and 1976) deserves mention, also, since he has completed a unique longitudinal study with the aim of identifying definite stages of language development. Although his findings are not different in character from the broad perspective of development already described, he was able to highlight one crucial problem. He found that the frequency of dependent clauses in the written language of high-ability 13 year olds did not increase thereafter while it did for low-ability children. This suggests, in effect, that there is a ceiling to the effectiveness of such frequency-counts. After a certain stage, children become able to use a greater variety of linguistic devices to express certain sorts of clausal relations and this makes them less reliant on dependent-clause structures. It is clear, therefore, that frequency-count indicators are useful only when investigating the development of immature writers. They are not of value in the description of mature ability, nor in the description of the demands of writing for specific purposes.

All of the research so far considered comes from the United States. A similar range of features was considered by Harpin (1976) in a project funded by the SSRC at Nottingham University. In brief, he reports that as children of average and above-average ability mature as writers they tend to produce writing of increasing length; they write longer and more complex sentences; they employ a greater variety of clause types; and they tend to use personal pronouns less. (All these findings are averages and do not relate to single pieces of work.) None of this information is, in fact, particularly surprising nor is it of great practical value in day-to-day teaching. What it provides – with many qualifications – is an outline of one aspect of development and an awareness that, at certain stages, certain types of writing will be difficult for children because of limitations in the range of syntactic features they can deploy.

Before moving on to look at the new developments that I suggested initially might constitute the basis for a redirection in writing, it is worth considering some of the shortcomings of the frequency-count approach just described. An obvious problem is that a text is not made up of collections of sentences, but of sentences organised into a coherent whole. To work merely at sentence level is to ignore crucially important aspects of text. With the exception of Hunt's work, all the other researchers have taken the sentence as broadly unproblematic. Harpin does, incidentally, offer working definitions for sentence division in a text that has multiple co-ordination (i.e. strings of clauses joined by *and* or *and so* or *and then*) which is, of course, a highly typical feature of the writing of children in junior schools. The sentence, however, cannot be taken for granted, as we shall see. Moreover, in all this research work there is a failure to differentiate types of writing adequately. Harpin, for example, follows the traditional primary curriculum model of writing, distinguishing only the creative and the factual, but admits that this a weakness in his work. Categorising types of writing is not easy, but there is good evidence to suggest that the type of writing attempted has a strong influence on the outcome. Above all, research of the kind described above is informative and helpful in some ways as a tool for looking with some objectivity at children's writing; but it does not isolate areas of difficulty or suggest teaching strategies to promote more effective writing. Bearing these points in mind, let us now turn our attention to new developments.

New developments

I want to suggest that there are three areas in which our understanding of writing has grown in recent years. These are:

1 the differences between speech and writing;
2 the nature and internal organisation of written texts;
3 the processes of writing – and concomitant with this, the appreciation that for the purposes of teaching, the process is of prior importance to the product.

Speech and writing

A study of how speech and writing have been viewed by linguistics provides an interesting, albeit indirect, perspective on the development of linguistics as a discipline. Schafer (1981) offers a useful historical survey in which he shows how the founding fathers of modern linguistics, de Saussure and Bloomfield, reacting against the total neglect of speech in the pre-existing traditions of rhetoric and grammar, asserted the primacy of speech. This emphasis was clearly crucial to the emerging discipline of linguistics, but has led to some strange distortions. One of these is the belief that (to use Bloomfield's words) 'writing is merely a way of recording language by means of visible marks', with the implication that it is, therefore, an inferior mode of communication. Another is that the methodology of transformational grammarians has obscured the need for investigation of speech-writing differences. By dealing only with idealised language instances – speech purged of irregularities such as hesitations or reformulations, of dialectal variation and of context-dependent features – they removed the necessity to account for differences between the two modes.

However, the increasing interest in *discourse* and *text analysis* over the last ten years has sharpened awareness of some crucial differences. This is because the emphasis has shifted from idealised language data to an examination of language-in-use.

I shall isolate six points of difference that seem to me important to our appreciation of why it is that children normally find writing difficult. In this discussion I am taking for granted certain obvious features. These include the different rates of production for speech, and writing, the degree of standardisation in writing as opposed to speech and the absence in writing of intonational features that can only be compensated for by sentence patterns which provide to a degree the emphases more readily available in speech. (See also Stubbs, 1980.)

Planning in speech and writing. In speech, particularly in informal conversation, we plan at the point of utterance – hence the hesitations, false starts, reformulations and so on that are part and parcel of the nature of speech and that deviate in frequency only when speech becomes either highly formalised (i.e. 'frozen', as Joos (1967) calls it) or highly intimate. Equally, much conversation has a regular pattern to it. Sinclair and Coulthard (1975) show that much of a child's experience of language in the classroom, in terms of teacher-pupil exchanges, is marked by a pattern of *Initiation – Response – Feedback*. The teacher asks the questions; the pupil supplies the answer; the teacher makes a confirming or dismissive comment or gesture.

Within this pattern, the responsibility for planning the shape of the discourse rests with the dominant partner – the teacher. So the pupil needs merely to work within the constraints of the set pattern and is usually concerned, in terms of planning, with the content of the utterance, not with its form. Even in less formalised exchanges, there is a high degree of mutuality in the development of a discourse which provides a considerable degree of support for the child.

By contrast, the writer is in sole control of the planning of the text. He or she has to generate both questions and answers, and in a well-organised text it is the generating of questions that is the most difficult task. These questions are not, of course, part of the finished text, but are internalised agencies in planning. Widdowson (1983) suggests that this planning process can be seen as a 'covert interaction' in which the writer plays the role of both the initiator and recipient of the discourse (i.e. speaker *and* hearer). The initiating, moreover, is not simply a matter of beginning the text, but of initiating each new unit of the text in a way that has regard both for what precedes and for what a reader needs to know.

Process of production. I have already suggested that in speech we normally plan at the point of utterance and that is evidenced in those typical features of speech which appear so surprising and, indeed, shocking to people inspecting transcripts for the first time. For instance, this is a transcript of the opening moments of a small group discussion of a poem

(*Postscript* by Louis MacNeice). The participants are first-
year college students. (I have added a minimum of punctuation, thus (?) or . . . indicates a pause.)

> Now we'll start at the beginning which is . . . er . . . that
> f-f-first two lines which is probably the most obvious
> well I think so anyway . . . er . . . mm when he says we
> were children words were coloured . . . er . . . and then in
> brackets . . . er . . . just as an aside sort of thing harlot and
> murder were dark purple why is harlot and especially
> murder dark purple(?) is that any reference to blood(?)
> (several voices)

C.   I think
D.   blood's not purple is it(?)
(laughter)
C.   Jeremy's is
J.   mine is
D.   thought it was red
S.   mixture of blue blood and ordinary blood
D.   I would say . . . well . . . purple's s'posed to
          be royal anyway
C. and S. yeh . . . mm
C.   but that might it of course the fact that . . .
          yeh . . . that . . . mm
J.   I was saving myself for that one
(laughter)
S.   that they were idealised
C.   no(.) that yeh . . . that they were . . . no . . . I
          wonder if it's purple royal it wasn't in contact
          with him it was something royal(.) you know
          how royal things are out of contact with ordi-
          nary people . . . mm
S.   yeh but
D.   yeh
C.   there were things that he only heard about
          from a distance(.) he wasn't actually tainted
          by things like harlot

J.   yeh but why throw it in as an aside sort of
          thing in brackets
C.   yeh
J.   I think it's more or less to – to . . . say you
          know . . . er . . . the . . . sort of colour scheme
          for various feelings

Three things stand out clearly that are relevant to the
present discussion. First, there is a great deal of hesitancy and
reformulation going on. The reformulations are there because
there is a ferment of thought in process, demanding words.
The thoughts are subject also to refinement within the
dynamic of the group. Second, no statement is fully preconsi-
dered. In a small group discussion, it would be inappropriate
and wasteful of valuable opportunities for interactive learning
if the participants sat in silence sorting out a considered
statement which each delivered when ready. Also there would
be no meeting of minds in such a procedure. Finally, the
impetus of the discussion is both forward and circular but not
in neat and tidy movements. There is no striving towards an
authoritative statement. Revisions of 'untidy' utterances tend
in themselves to be untidy too. This, of course, gives rise to
the often-remarked feature of discussions that, while their
coherence will be clear to the participants, they are far from
clear to the detached viewer/reader looking at a transcript and
not in tune with the immediate situation.

If, then, we revise speech as we go along – just prior in fact
to the production of the sound stream – the production
process in writing is much more complex. To point the
contrast, we can look at the process of written production in
action through a piece of writing by a 10 year old, Thomas.
Initially we have a set of notes (see figure 5.1). It is the first
stage of a lengthy process of writing. The work that prompted
the writing began when the teacher brought into the class (a
combined J3/J4 class) a piece of driftwood she had been
given. Over a period of time, groups of children examined the
wood, looking at its texture and shape, measuring it and
examining samples of the wood and other matter attached to

D

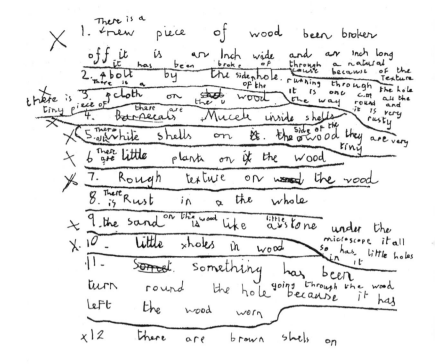

Figure 5.1

the wood under the microscope. They made rough notes as they did this.

There are some points of interest in Thomas's notes. In each he jots down an initial point – '1. new piece of wood been broken off; 2. bolt by the hole; 3. cloth on wood; 4. mucels (sic) inside shells'; and so on. On each of these points he is able to expand as the result of more detailed observation into which he also introduces his own speculations, as in 'it has been broke of [sic] through a natural cause because of the texture'. It is because he is concerned only with a private set of notes that he is able to enrich his initial comments in this way. He is also able at a later stage to add bits of language that move his notes towards sentence form – 'There is a', for

instance, in point 1. From the teaching point of view, it is
worth noting that Thomas is not under the pressure that
children normally face in school of having to get their first
thoughts down on paper in a finished, final form. As he adds
detail he records it simply to his own satisfaction and in a
form adequate to his own purposes. He is able, also, to work
on his notes towards a more publicly acceptable form of
language. But he does not have to cope with all of this all at
once.

The next stage is shown in figure 5.2. Thomas had decided
that in his piece of writing he would set out his speculations
on the history of the piece of wood. The piece starts quite
confidently as a 'narrative with an elaborated setting' (I am
using the terminology of Labov and Waletsky, 1967). When
he comes to the first dramatic event he appears to be reaching
towards a dramatic present *here comes* but is constrained by
the prevailing past tense of the narration. The playing with
words to achieve effect in the description of the progress of
the wave is fascinating. And in the last section of the piece,
because he knows that he is writing a draft, Thomas is able to
add detail, to experiment with his choice of words, to cut out
and to insert. This is, indeed, a valuable example of a young
writer thinking on paper. The process, it should be clear, is
very much more than 'recording language by means of visible
marks'.

Here is Thomas's final piece, which is presented in
type because the original was written on a large piece of paper
and integrated with a beautiful line drawing of the piece of
wood. Along with other contributions from the class, it was
mounted for display in the school. The whole process lasted,
intermittently, for several days.

A piece of wood

The harbour wall was made of solid concrete in fact the
only thing that wasn't concrete was the wood that ran
down the harbour wall. The waves were crashing down

Wave breaker

The waves were crashing down, rising into the air then smashing against the water below spreading the beach with a white spray. (father) Further up the beach it was all quiet the only thing was a line of wave breakers, they all looked the same, They all had a iron stakes in (nobody knew why they were there they just were). Another thing, they all had were mussels every where you looked on a breaker there were clusters of muscles. All this time the tide was coming in and now was smashing against wave breakers but every wave was smashed. But here came a big wave.

it started out as a little ripple in then the sea became it quite bigger and bigger an enormous wave it rose in the air and smashed against the breaker, the breaker broke into two. After that the tide slowly went out, with it the piece of wood. The wood floated for weeks, Through that it got a very funny texture. The wood finally landed on a beach in Hornsea, Then Were a man picked it up and drove off with it. (On the wood there was some ruts I think these where made by some animal)

the wood is sort of very rough in some parts and there are lots of tiny holes in the wood the worms drilled through then before it was broken in two

& as it floated some plants became got caught in the wood and slowly it floated the roots get inbeded themselves in the wood and they began to grow there.

Figure 5.2 Wave breaker

rising into the air, then crashing against the water below, spreading the beach with a white spray. Further up the beach it was all quiet the thing there was a line of wave breakers. they all looked the same, they all had iron stakes in, they were there to strengthen the breaker in case a big wave came. Another thing they all had were mussels, everywhere you looked on a breaker there were clusters of mussels. All the time the tide was coming and now was smashing against the wave breakers, but here came a big wave. It started out as a little ripple in the sea then it became an enormous wave it rose into the air then smashed against the breaker, the breaker broke into two. After that the tide went slowly out, with it the piece of wood. The wood floated for many weeks, through the many days at sea many things happened like the strange shape it had formed from being slashed off by the sea. The sea had worn little ruts in the wood and barnacles were clinging to it everywhere. As it floated some plants became caught in the wood and the roots inbeded themselves and began to grow there. Also the wood formed a very strange texture, it is very rough in patches and there are lots of tiny holes in the wood where worms had tunnelled there before it was broken off. The wood finally landed on a beach in Hornsea where a man picked it up and drove off with it.

Not every piece of work a child undertakes needs to proceed through successive stages of drafting. There are many children, for example, who are able and fluent story writers. For them the demand to draft or revise a long story would be wholly inappropriate. Moreover, if we make indiscriminate use of drafting, if it is invariably or artificially imposed, it may well lead to a child's interest in writing declining. This must be avoided at all costs.

We should also remember that just as not every piece of writing need go through one or more stages of drafting, so some pieces of writing need not be pursued to a finished stage. It will depend on the purpose of, and audience for, the writing. It is also worth noting that there are several teaching points that could usefully be made at a draft stage in Thomas's work, notably the need to review the time sequence of the verbs in the penultimate sentence.

The remaining points must be considered more briefly.

The text and the context. I suggested that the transcript of the discussion of *Postscript* is difficult to comprehend, yet the discussion was a perfectly intelligible, even exhilarating, experience for the participants. The question of context has a lot to do with this. Speech is constrained by the situation in which it is produced and needs only to be appropriate to it. The degree of constraint and of dependency varies with the type of communicative context. Writing, however, needs to communicate beyond the immediate, often to a relatively unknown audience. In this sense it aspires to being context-free. This is apparent in the differing uses of deixis (pointing) in speech and writing. In speech we frequently use reference words such as the demonstratives *this* and *that* or the personal pronouns, *he*, *she*, *it* to point to persons or objects present and therefore known to the participants. In writing, these words need a point of reference already established in the text. The 12 year old who started an account of a woodwork project by writing 'When I made it I used glue and a tennon saw' failed to appreciate that *it* had not been established *textually*. If he had included a title such as *My letter-rack* then the identity of *it* would become clear. Such 'context-bound' features in children's writing have sometimes been explained in terms of Bernstein's codes. It seems to me, however, that to view them as part of a wider set of problems relating to speech-writing differences is more consistent with verifiable linguistic data. Teachers need to be aware of the different contextual constraints on speaking and on writing and build these perceptions into their teaching strategies.

The syntax of speech and writing.   One of the most dramatic areas of difference between speech and writing is found in the typical syntax of the two modes. Kress (1982) states the position clearly:

> The sentence is not a unit of typical spoken language. The sentence belongs to writing, forming there the basic unit of textual structures. The sentence may occur in speech as a borrowing from the syntax of writing, but speech, typically, is organised on the basis of clausal complexes which are not sentences. They may be long chains of clauses linked by co-ordination or simply by being adjoined. While the sentence typically is a structure of main and subordinated and embedded clauses, the clausal complex is typically an aggregate rather than a syntactic structure.

The insistence in this quotation on typicality shows that the difference is not an absolute one in the sense that speech has one grammar and writing another. It is rather that there is a fundamental difference in the distribution of syntactic features between the two modes. Speech tends to loosely co-ordinated structures; writing to hierarchically organised structures. This is of great significance to our understanding of children as writers. It means, for instance, that learning to write is, in part, a process of coming to understand the nature of the sentence as a linguistic unit.

A careful look, for instance, at the way that punctuation is used in the final version of *A Piece of Wood* suggests that there is some loosely conceived principle of grouping together thematically related information or events rather than any rigorous application of sentence delineation according to syntactic groupings.

Reductionism and elaboration.   Closely related to the question of syntax is another feature of difference that has only recently become clear, as linguists have studied 'real' as opposed to idealised language data. Descriptions of conversational exchanges usually draw attention to what linguists term 'ellipsis'. Halliday and Hasan (1976) define it thus: 'An elliptical item is one which, as it were, leaves specific structural slots to be filled from elsewhere.' Typically, we find ellipsis occurring in exchanges like this:

> Are you going to the theatre tonight?
> No. Tomorrow.

Tomorrow is usually explained as *I am going to the theatre tomorrow* but with all the slots elided except the adjunct *tomorrow*. It may, however, be more useful to think of *No. Tomorrow.* as the norm for conversational speech; that is, to accept that in informal speech there is an inherent tendency to a reductionism by which we say only that which is necessary to effective communication. It is, then, not so much a case of ellipsis occurring in informal speech as of writing requiring a degree of elaboration that is not necessary in informal speech. Again, I would suggest that the degree of elaboration required in written text is a feature children need to come to terms with at school. It is a way of thinking and expressing oneself in language that is radically different from conversational speech.

Speech, writing and audience.   When we talk to someone, we either already know or quickly establish areas of shared knowledge and experience. Where there appears to be a mismatch, this is usually appreciated pretty well instantaneously because the speaker receives immediate feedback from the conversational partner. Writers, however, do not have the benefit of immediate feedback. They may receive feedback from those to whom they are willing and able to show the text at a draft stage. They may also receive some comments post-publication. Nevertheless, at the point of writing, their perception of their readership is an important facet of their ability as writers. Moffett (1968) relates the development of reader-awareness in children to a general developmental tendency he terms 'decentring' – a move away from a preoccupation with the self, the present and the immediate. The notion of reader-awareness seems to me much more powerful than Britton's audience categories, which are difficult to verify and have no validity outside the school context.

The organisation of written text

I have suggested that one of the difficulties facing a writer is the posing of questions that in a sense underpin the surface of the text. That is only part of the story. The statement begs the question of what form these questions should take. Clearly there is a difference between a story or personal reminiscence on the one hand, where the obvious question is 'What happened next?', and, on the other hand, an essay on 'Democracy versus Dictatorship'. In the latter case there is no clear set of questions to be asked, though they might include 'What is democracy? How does it differ from dictatorship? What are the advantages/disadvantages of either?' Inherent in the type of question posed is a fundamental distinction between two major forms of organisation of written texts – the time-related and the non-time-related.

Time-related organisation. Text organisation is an area of study very much in its infancy, yet interesting pointers are emerging both in relation to reading and to writing (see, for instance, Byron et al., 1981 and Hoey, 1983). My own investigation into the organisation of written texts at lower secondary level (Harris, 1980) points to the occurrence of a range of sharply differentiated linguistic features that vary not so much with subject areas but with what appear to be fundamental text types. As yet, however, no rigorous taxonomy of text types is available, let alone describable in terms of typical linguistic features. What follows is offered as a tentative approach, but one that has already proved useful to teachers.

1 Fictional narrative. Unless a writer chooses to manipulate a narrative for particular effects, such as using flashbacks, the progression of events in a narrative text is dictated by the progression of events in the imagined world of the story. Young children appear to acquire a 'grammar' of story comparatively early and are able to deal with the sequencing with reasonable success – i.e. the initial events are sequenced initially in the text and so on. Later sophistications follow, such as balance between more and less essential events, between setting and events and, ultimately, the plotting of events to form some overall shape and to give a sense of resolution to the narrative. Fictional narratives, then, are an obvious example of time-related writing.

2   Personal narratives. Personal narratives or short autobiographical pieces function organisationally in much the same way as fictional narratives, except that the writer is constrained by existential rather than imagined events. Yet in both types of narrative the basic question the writer has to ask to establish the next unit of text is 'What happened next?' I start, for example, with an initial event:

> Yesterday, I arrived home just after dark. It was a wet, blustery evening.

The second sentence constitutes part of the setting along with the time elements established in the first sentence. How do I know what to write next? I ask myself what happened next and if it is significant to the narrative.

> I felt in my pocket for my door key.

What happened next?

> I could not find it.

At this minimal level, narrative is organisationally simple and, linguistically, cohesion will tend to be established by time

clauses (*when* . . .), time connectors (*next* . . .) and pronomi-
nalisations (John . . . *he,* or door-key. . . *it,* in the last
example). Problems are likely to occur if there are several
'actors' in the story – if, that is, the story is about Tom, Dick
and Harry, rather than just William, for then simple
pronominalisation is not always possible without ambiguity.
Crystal (1979) demonstrates this in his valuable analysis of a
piece of personal reminiscence by a 9 year old.

3 Quasi-narrative. Interestingly enough, there are several
types of writing commonly practised in school that are
organised on a time-related basis, yet are not strictly
narratives. Descriptions of historical events, of scientific
processes, of processes related to home economics or craft,
design and technology work, for instance, all require that the
writer recalls 'what happened next' or, in a generalising sense,
'what happens next'.

Non-time-related. What happens, however, when the 'What
happened next?' question is not appropriate? Certainly there
will be no ground-plan in reality to which the writer can refer
to discover a basis for organising the text. Some non-time-
related texts are organised on a classificatory basis, some on a
comparison-contrast, others on a hypothesising basis. (For a
discussion of the linguistic features of comparison-contrast
see Hoey, 1983, and Harris, 1980, 1985, in press). Several
analysts have also shown that a 'problem-solution' pattern is
commonly found, particularly in scientific texts. Such a
pattern, however, may be organised on a time-related basis.

An example may serve best at this stage to illustrate
something of the range of problems often encountered by
pupils when composing non-time-related texts.

The example for analysis from an organisational perspective is a piece of fourth year secondary biology writing. The
task set was to write an essay on *Reflex Actions* and, as a rider,
to include an account of the reflex pathway followed when a
person puts a hand on a pin. It is, incidentally, interesting to
note that such a hybrid form (two separate topics in one

'essay') is highly typical of the school essay and, at the same time, highly untypical of anything found in 'real-world' writing. Here is the text in full. It is a particularly successful version compared with those produced by other pupils in the group who were set the task. The sentences are numbered for ease of reference. (Paragraph indentations occur between sentences 6 and 7 and 7 and 8.)

1   Reflex actions are processes which occur within the body and are important to us in that they sometimes prevent us being seriously injured.

2   A reflex action is a response to a stimulus which occurs extremely quickly and does not require conscious thought.

3   This is because the impulses from the stimulus have only to travel to the spinal cord and not the brain.

4   Some reflex actions have to be learnt such as tying a shoe lace, chewing a pencil under stress and biting nails, but others come naturally from the moment we are born like digestion, breathing and jerking our big toe out of the bath water when we have forgotten to turn the cold tap on.

5   This latter fact forms the dividing line between the two categories of reflex action.

6   These are:
(a) conditioned which must be learnt and are our habits, personal to ourselves;
(b) inborn which are instinctive and common to everyone.

7   The following reflex pathway is the route along which impulses travel when we prick our hand on a sharp pin.

8   The stimulus is the pin which when pressed onto the hand, causes us to feel pain.

9   This pain is then converted into a nervous impulse which travels very rapidly along the sensory nerve towards the spinal cord.

10 It enters the spinal cord through the dorsal root of the spinal nerve from where it passes through the white matter and into the grey matter.

11 Here, the impulse jumps across the synapse between the sensory neurone and the connector neurone via the acetyl choline in the middle.

12 The same chemical is responsible for transferring the impulse to the neurone.

13 The motor neurone then leads the impulse out of the grey matter, the white matter and the ventral root of the spinal nerve.

14 The impulse finally arrives at the biceps by means of the motor end plate.

15 It causes the muscle to contract and hence the hand is pulled away from the pin.

The first major point is that the text is basically in two parts: sentences 1-6 and sentences 7-15. The first part is organised on a non-time-related basis, the second part is basically time-related in that the principle for determining the content of any subsequent sentence is 'what does the nervous impulse do next?' The time-related organisation is realised, in part, through the use of temporal connectors *then, then* and *finally*. In essence, the description of the reflex pathway is a miniature narrative but *generalised* as a *typical* activity by the use of the *present* tense whereas a fictional narrative is almost invariably reported in the *past* tense.

In common also with the simple narrative is the use of pronominalisation for mentions, subsequent to the initial one, of the main agent of the action – here the nervous impulse which is replaced by *it*. The exception to this is in sentences 11-14 where we find the locational reference *here* and functional reference *the same chemical is responsible for . . .* This point is highly significant and not just in relation to the text under discussion.

At one extreme, the description of the reflex pathway can be regarded as an account of a 'real-time' journey of the impulses from the pain receptor along the sensory fibres to the spinal cord and back along the motor fibres to the biceps muscle. At the other extreme, we may consider the required description (which is, after all, that of a *pathway*, not a *journey*) to be locational and functional. In simple abstract form these two extremes may be represented thus:

1 *Real-time journey* of impulse = a, where x, y and z represent parts of the nervous system.

a stimulated by pain $\rightarrow$ along x $\rightarrow$ through y $\rightarrow$ returns along z $\rightarrow$ muscle

2 *Locational and functional* pain produces a by effector w; w is linked to x; x is connected to y; y performs such and such a function; z is connected to y and linked to muscle; x, y and z constitute the pathway for a.

In essence, number 1 is no different to the way we habitually give directions to people. In answer to the question 'where is the White House?', we tend to respond with a step-by-step description of the journey to be taken. We organise our answer on a time-related basis. Indeed, it might be ventured that whenever there is the possibility we prefer to use this basis of organisation, probably because it is intrinsically more accessible and more firmly established as part of our mental 'set'.

However, the main point of interest is the first part of the text. The accompanying table (see table 5.1) sets out the main features of how the text is organised. The crucial point is that the non-time-related organisation requires a conceptual grasp of the content and a level of linguistic ability which allows the writer to realise the concepts successfully in the text. In this particular case the underlying concept is a classification of reflex actions into two types – the conditioned (CRA) and the inborn (IRA). These two are compared – classifications involve comparisons and contrasts – and the mechanism of the comparison is that the two types (CRAs and IRAs) are matched together, but always against a further factor.

Table 5.1 Organisation in the first part of the biology text

Text item	Comment
Sentence 1 Reflex Actions are processes . . .	Generalised definition of value of RAs to human beings
Sentence 2 A Reflex Action is . . .	Specific definition of the operation of a RA
Sentence 3 This is because . . .	Reason for operation described in S2, here separated into a further sentence although part of the same 'idea unit'. Sentence linkage is realised in a sophisticated manner by use of nominal *This* and subordinator indicating 'reason'
Sentence 4 Some Reflex Actions . . . but others . . .	Broad classification established by comparison which is realised in lexical items *some . . . other*. Difference (contrast) emphasised by conjunction *but*
Sentence 5 This latter fact . . .	Principle of categorisation signalled by *dividing line* . . .
Sentence 6 These are (a) . . . (b) . . .	. . . and realised in two-fold definition fulfilling expectation set up in S5

Conceptually, this is a complex process requiring what Piaget termed a 'formal operational' stage of cognitive development. Linguistically, it requires the ability to deploy a sophisticated range of text organisational devices.

As a comparison, here are two examples from the same set of children of how things can go wrong in the expression of comparison.

1 A Reflex Action is a rapid response (automatic) to a stimulus by an organ which does not involve the brain for its initiation.
2 Many reflexes involve only the impulse passing through the spinal cord, not the brain.
3 Reflexes control many of our important functions such as breathing and digestion.
4 Reflex Actions may be inborn, being present at our birth already given to us.
5 *They* are acquired during an individual's lifetime.

In this version the broad categorisation of a) IRAs and b) CRAs is not present in the text. However, in S4-5 the contrast is implied. *They* (S5) needs to be understood as replacing 'conditioned reflex actions'. As written, the text involves a contradiction. *They* replaces *Reflex Actions* (S4) to which, in fact, it needs to stand in contrast.

1 A Reflex Action is a process in the body which needs no thought to happen.
2 It responses [sic] to a stimulus which occurs very quickly.
3 The quickness of this action is because the impulses do not have to travel to the brain, only the spinal cord.
4 Reflex Actions control our natural and important functions, e.g. breathing and blinking.
5 *But other* Reflex Actions may be inborn or conditioned.
6 *These* actions have to be learnt.
7 And inborn are instinctive and common to everyone.
8 The unnatural actions are such as tying a shoe lace and biting nails.

Sentence 5 is the pivot sentence in the comparison: *but* and *other* are the lexical items that explicitly realise the comparison. However, the two items being compared are both present in S5, *inborn* and *conditioned*. Consequently, in S6 the identity signal *these*, while it should be confirming the co-referentiality of *actions* with 'conditioned reflex actions', in fact co-refers with *other Reflex Actions*.

These last two examples raise important questions of assessment. Are we to infer from the texts that the pupils do not understand the differences between inborn and conditioned reflexes? It is, to my mind, probable in both cases that it is the written expression of this understanding that is at fault. The teaching has given the pupils the necessary facts but not the help to consolidate understanding in writing (or indeed in talk), nor to master the compositional abilities to realise the understanding successfully.

The process of writing

It seems beyond question that any sensible approach to the teaching of writing has to take account of the process of writing. Indeed, one of the most serious deficiencies in much classroom practice is the total lack of perception that writing can rarely be a once-off activity and, at the same time, a successful one. Barnes and Shemilt (1974) term this practice *first-draft final-draft writing*, indicating, memorably, that most classroom practice of writing involves a distortion of the real-world experience of serious writing. Yet investigations of the writing process suggest that there is more than one way to salvation and that what suits one pupil may well hinder another – the protracted act of discovery and experiment that Thomas was engaged in with his piece of wood writings may well be a complete turn-off for another child. Because of the limitations of research in this difficult area there is a tendency in work addressed to teachers for complexities to be overlooked. Marshall (1974), for instance, insists on the necessity for a period of 'scrambling' (others call it 'gestation') between the experience or stimulus and the writing.

More recently, and particularly in America, the *conference-drafting* approach to teaching writing has become fashionable. The terminology is self-explanatory. Pupils are encouraged, even expected, to pursue a topic through several drafts before editing for publication in whatever local sense this may occur. At each stage – prior to drafting as well as at the end of each stage of drafting – teachers confer with pupils. The classroom becomes a writing workshop. Much of the approach appears consistent with our understanding of how mature writers function. Yet there are worries. Descriptions of the approach betray a degree of systematisation that elevates the system above the pupil. It is difficult, too, to see how such an approach could be happily integrated into a balanced curriculum. Writing thus approached becomes an end in itself. Nor is it evident that the results are successful. Graves (1983), in what purports to be a major study of the conference-drafting approach, fails to show the process at work. Nor does he consider the possibility that some pupils may find that the approach does not work for them. There is, of course, always a danger in generalising from individual writing. It may well be that as, perhaps, in the teaching of reading, so in the teaching of writing, the real art lies in discerning the approach that best suits the individual writer for a particular type of compositional task. A genuine collaboration between pupil and teacher would then be forged.

Nevertheless, it does seem reasonable to suggest that teachers need to be aware that when tackling many writing tasks pupils will achieve a greater degree of success, both as writers and as learners, if they can work in stages, and if within these stages they have sympathetic and informed support from both teachers and peers – not, I would insist, seeking to impose a preconceived notion of how to plan or how to write, but helping pupils to discover what works best for them.

Conclusions

I suggested initially that a quiet revolution was taking place in the study of writing, so perhaps it will then be a disappointment at the end of the chapter to stress that there are no easy solutions to questions of classroom practice. It may be that work since the mid-seventies, valuable as much of it is, has in fact done no more than to clarify how much more we need to investigate and to highlight what we should always have known – that writing and the teaching of writing are immensely complex activities. Nevertheless, I will venture some concluding statements.

1   The questioning of the place and function of writing in both the primary and secondary curricula needs to continue. The sheer quantity of writing set in school may well be creating unthinking and ineffective writers.

2   There needs to be greater attention to process in writing, though there is a danger that this can become an end in itself. (I'm reminded of Grand in Camus' *La Peste* who spent a life-time refining the opening sentence of his novel!) And, certainly, we cannot assume that processes in writing are unvarying. A reasonable starting point may be to assume that the process will vary for individuals and for different types of text.

3   There needs to be a major initiative to raise consciousness about the nature of writing and written text. It is interesting to see that some developments in reading instruction are stressing the need to help pupils cope with text organisational problems. There is here a useful area of cross-fertilisation between reading and writing which should be greatly helpful to pupils as writers.

4   Teachers as the main providers of response to children's writing need to become better readers. This entails both a greater awareness of text features and provision of more time for reading. Scan readings alongside the child in the classroom probably reveal only deviations such as errors in spelling

(automatically condemned, but not analysed) or unusual expressions (usually praised in 'creative' work even if highly inappropriate to the total effect of the text).

5 There needs to be a greater appreciation that writing is a distinct mode of language use. Children have to learn competence in this mode in terms of its syntax, its organisational patterns and its contextual constraints – much as if it were a second language. Clearly it is not, but the hyperbole is a useful corrective to some of the simplistic notions presently informing the teaching of writing such as 'If they have something interesting to say, they'll get it down all right.'

References

Barnes, D. and Shemilt, D. (1974) 'Transmission and Interpretation', *Educational Review*, 26, 213-28.
Bereiter, C. (1980) 'Development in Writing', in Gregg, L. and Steinberg, E. (eds), *Cognitive Processes in Writing*. Erlbaum.
Britton, J., Burgess, T., Martin, M., McLeod, A. and Rosen, H. (1975) *The Development of Writing Abilities 11-18*. Macmillan.
Byron, D., Davies, F., Gardner, K., Greene, T. and Lunzer, E. (1981) 'Reading to learn.' Paper presented to the International Reading Association, New Orleans.
Crystal, D. (1979) 'Language in education – a linguistic perspective', in Cashdan, A. (ed.), *Language, Reading and Learning*. Basil Blackwell.
DES (1975) *A Language for Life* (The Bullock report). HMSO.
DES (1978) *Primary Education in England*. HMSO.
DES (1979) *Aspects of Secondary Education in England*. HMSO.
Galton, M. et al. (1980) *Inside the Primary Classroom*. Routledge & Kegan Paul.
Graves, D. (1983) *Writing: Teachers and Children at Work*. Heinemann.
Halliday, M. and Hasan, R. (1976) *Cohesion in English*. Longman.
Harpin, W. (1976) *The Second 'R'*. Allen & Unwin.
Harris, J. (1980) 'Suprasentential Organisation in Written Discourse with Particular Reference to Writing by Children in the Lower Secondary Age-range'. MA thesis, University of Birmingham.
Harris, J. (1985, in press) 'Organisation in children's writing', in Harris, J. and Wilkinson, J., *Reading Children's Writing*. Allen & Unwin.
Hoey, M. (1983) *On the Surface of Discourse*. Allen & Unwin.
Hunt, W. K. (1965) *Grammatical Structures Written at Three Grade Levels*, Research Report No. 3. National Council for the Teaching of English (NCTE).

Joos, M. (1967) *The Five Clocks*. Harcourt Brace Jovanovich.

Kress, G. (1982) *Learning to Write*. Routledge & Kegan Paul.

Labov, W. and Waletsky, J. (1967) 'Oral versions of personal experience', in Helm, J. (ed.), *Essays on the Verbal and Visual Arts*. University of Washington Press.

La Brant, L. (1933) 'A study of certain language developments in children', *Genetic Psychology Monographs, 14*.

Loban, W. (1963) *The Language of Elementary School Children*, Research Report No. 1. NCTE.

Loban, W. (1976) *Language Development: Kindergarten through Grade Twelve*, Research Report No. 18. NCTE.

Marshall, S. (1974) *Creative Writing*. Macmillan.

Moffett, J. (1968) *Teaching the Universe of Discourse*. Houghton Mifflin.

Schafer, J. (1981) 'The linguistic analysis of spoken and written texts', in Kroll, B. and Vann, R. (eds), *Explaining Speaking-Writing Relationships*. NCTE.

Sinclair, J. and Coulthard, M. (1975) *Towards an Analysis of Discourse*. Oxford University Press.

Stubbs, M. (1980) *Language and Literacy*. Routledge & Kegan Paul.

Whitehead, F.S. (1978) 'What's the use, indeed?', *The Use of English, 29*, 15-22.

Widdowson, H. (1983) 'New starts and different kinds of failure', in Freedman, A., Pringle, I. and Yalden, J. (eds), *Learning to Write: First Language/Second Language*. Longman.

Williams, J. (1977) *Learning to Write or Writing to Learn*. National Foundation for Educational Research (NFER).

6

Hearing children read

Helen Arnold

It may appear curiously anachronistic to include a chapter on 'hearing children read' in a book which looks forward to language and learning in an age of computers and mechanisation. The title implies an over-concentration on the minutiae of classroom pedagogy when what may be considered really important are broad issues of curriculum development. Its inclusion may be justified, however, on two main counts. Listening to children reading has dominated the early stages of reading instruction for several decades, and still does to a great extent. More importantly, close examination of the practice uncovers fundamental issues which are beginning to seep through from the pages of research journals to the consciousness of many individual teachers in the classroom, and to affect the way they see their role. The strongly held belief that the teaching of reading is the sole prerogative of the professional (together with a tenacious preservation of its mystiques) has been accepted for years. Now the ripples of self-doubt have become a groundswell, and it seems worthwhile to trace why and how radical changes in methodology have begun to take effect. This chapter will begin with a brief survey of 'hearing children read' as it has been popularly practised. It will then suggest influences which have led to its reconsideration, finally looking towards future developments.

Present practice

Many teachers – and parents – believe that the core of mastering reading skill lies only in individual contact between adult and child. The text used in this contact is invariably the 'basic' reading scheme, referred to as the 'reading book' by all concerned. For the child, 'real' reading is learnt from this particular book. In reality, the exercise is often ritualistic, and there is little evidence of genuine learning or teaching during the activity, for two main reasons. First, the child rarely encounters major difficulties in such reading, as the readability level of the text is supposedly geared to his or her stage of development. Second, the teacher is constantly interrupted by other children and cannot give full attention to the reader. This pattern has been documented in several research accounts of the primary classroom (e.g. Boydell 1978, Southgate, Arnold and Johnson, 1981). Instances have been cited of two or more children (six, in one teacher's account), reading aloud simultaneously to a teacher, each child from a different book. More typically, the individual child stands at the teacher's desk, muttering or stentoriously chanting for a few minutes, until checked by the ticking of a card which is slipped into the reading book at the page he or she has reached, or is expected to reach 'by next time'. Sometimes the child is warned not to go beyond the specified page until the next interview.

Margaret Spencer reported on a discussion held at a Schools Council Language for Learning Project Conference in 1981, when teachers were asked the question 'Why do we ask children to read to us?' Their responses included:

> They may expect it of us.
> It is one legitimised occasion of contact with an individual child.
> We may think we are monitoring how they are getting on.

We can ask ourselves if they are getting the meaning.
We can give the young reader a second opinion on what
is being read.

It is evident that the main emphases here are either on the
value of the practice for checking achievement (from the
teacher's angle), or on factors which are not directly related to
reading at all. The answers reflect the prevailing attitudes
towards hearing oral reading as a means of practising the skill
of reading in an asymmetrical relationship, with little
cognisance of the possibility of sharing the activity
collaboratively.

Robin Campbell (1981) has investigated this teacher-child
interaction. He found that positive feedback was predictably
given most often for accuracy and quantity of reading. He
also found that in many instances children were able to
correct their own errors when their attention was drawn to
them. When 'comprehension moves' were made they were
most frequently noted at the end of a read, although there was
often no follow-up on understanding text at all.

Gulliver (1979), investigating infant teachers' assumptions
in listening to reading, argued that the ploys that teachers
used in helping children read aloud were patterned by their
underlying perceptions of reading. Although he found that
teachers used many different strategies in helping children,
individuals tended to employ a limited range of reinforce-
ments and corrections according to whether they thought of
reading as a 'word-recognition skill' or a 'meaning-getting
process'. Teachers' perceptions about reading instruction
often derive from a pragmatic approach rather than from a
theoretical background. One teacher described to a group
how on his first day of teaching he faced his class of first-year
juniors thinking 'Reading? What do I do?' What he did was to
copy the practices that he observed within his school. He
described how it was only after four years' teaching that he
had begun to question what he was doing on the grounds of
both commonsense and increasing knowledge. Thus it can be

seen how a practice which has little educational validity can become a universal phenomenon.

The influences which are changing the practice of hearing children read come from several sources, but probably the most important is the effect of psycholinguistics, leading to a changed concept of the reading process. Frank Smith's (1971) seminal work, *Understanding Reading*, has been glorified and vilified perhaps more than any other book about reading, but it has spawned real excitement and self-questioning in teachers. The psycholinguist's interest in the processes at work in the reader's mind, rather than in the text itself, pushes into the forefront the need for the active involvement of the learner. Reading is a problem-solving activity, necessitating an active engagement with the text, an expectation of meaning, and the use of all cueing systems – grapho-phonemic, syntactic and semantic. Attitudes and motivation are more important than the ability to learn and apply rules dogmatically. 'The way in which learning to read is experienced by the child will determine how he will view learning in general, how he will conceive of himself as a person.' (Bettelheim and Zelan, 1982)

This view of the reading process is beginning to affect the nature of listening to children read. First, one begins to question the need for frequent rote regurgitation of words which lack intrinsic interest. Second, one sees the need to observe the act of reading aloud with much more precision, in order to diagnose the strategies which the reader is using. It is preferable to encourage those strategies which indicate a groping after meaning (contextual hypotheses) rather than those which show a grasp of surface features only. One does this best by collaborating with the child, by discussing his or her difficulties and successes, and by talking about the contents of the book. So the practice itself becomes useful for two different purposes, *diagnosis* and *collaboration*, which will probably not happen on the same occasion. The diagnostic purpose is particularly important and is best exemplified by a discussion of miscue analysis.

Miscue analysis

Miscue analysis is a way of listening to children read aloud for diagnostic purposes, originated by Kenneth Goodman (1969), and incorporating a psycholinguistic approach. The reading of a text, which will be difficult enough to produce errors, is tape-recorded and the reader's deviations from the original, known as miscues, are coded and analysed. The aim is to find how far the reader is using positive strategies, exemplified by certain types of miscue. In its original form, it is a time-consuming and complicated procedure, but it can be simplified so long as the underlying principles are honoured (see Arnold, 1982).

Doubts have recently arisen as to the value of miscue analysis, both in theory and as a viable practice for teachers (see, for example, Potter 1980). It remains to a great extent subjective and may therefore be open to disagreement in analysis. Researchers have found it hard to establish clear patterns of development, either in observing one child or in comparing different stages of reading mastery. Nor is it clear how well strategies shown in silent reading correlate with strategies used in reading aloud, a connection which is an underlying assumption in miscue analysis.

Despite these doubts, miscue analysis has much that is positive to commend it, and its increasing use is producing interesting sidelights for both teachers and pupils. Some useful generalisations have emerged:

1 Although individuals vary, there does seem to be a general developmental pattern revealed by miscue analysis:
   (a) About 6+ (reading ability, or RA) – the use of context at the expense of phonics. Children will remember and repeat chunks of text, linked with 'making up' parts of the story from picture clues. They begin to remember and use 'story language',

perhaps from previous stories read to them, and to exploit it in 'reading' new narrative material.

(b) About 8–9 (RA) – a preoccupation with the grapho-phonemic level, but making many substitutions which are syntactically appropriate. An increase in self-corrections. Decrease in non-responses.

(c) About 9+ (RA) – an ability to make substitutions which demonstrate cueing on all three levels. An increased use of omissions and insertions which do not affect the sense, indicating mental processing of the text before verbalisation. A decreasing number of self-corrections, showing that unconsciously made miscues are often semantically acceptable and do not need correction. Use of natural intonation rather than word-by-word chanting.

2 Biemiller's classic research (1970) into the 'development of the use of graphic and contextual information as children learn to read' isolated a plateau at about 8–9 years when children were shown to over-use the grapho-phonemic level. This has been confirmed in England; for example by a teacher in Manchester who believed it was caused in her sample by a phonic bias in the teaching. The same tendency to concentrate on grapho-phonemic cues has, however, been demonstrated by other children who had not had predominantly phonic training. Much appears to rest on the attitudes of the children themselves. At this age they tend to think that the way into reading must be by 'sounding the word out', and that 'guessing' is wrong. Whether their attitudes derive partly from the emphasis given to reading aloud is not proven.

3 Miscue analysis shows that although children attach great importance to the grapho-phonemic level, many of them do not actually use phonic tactics well. They frequently equate the first phoneme only with the graphic display, and then apply configuration and context cues, or merely wild guessing, to the rest of the

word. As Potter (1980) points out, it is difficult to differentiate from analysis how far morphemic or graphic cueing has influenced the response to the end of a word. We do see, however, through the examination of miscues, that children could become more consciously aware of the strategies they are *actually* using, rather than those which they (and the teacher) *think* they are using.

4 Different strategies are often seen at work in children of different chronological ages but with the same reading age. Less able older readers tend to perseverate with grapho-phonemic approximations, whereas the younger, better readers use more mature strategies. This has been interestingly investigated by Francis (1982).

5 When children are asked for free recall of what they have just read, (advocated by Goodman, 1969), younger children often read a difficult passage fluently, but are unable to tap the different levels of meaning (see below).

Teachers in the classroom are more likely to use miscue analysis for individual diagnosis rather than for the detection of broad developmental patterns. Considering the time it takes initially to carry out an analysis, it is quite surprising that a great deal of interest has been aroused. The reason may lie in what happens to the teachers themselves when they first encounter it, rather than in the use they make of it directly with children over a long period. Experience on inservice courses and in initial training shows that the real advantages go beyond hearing the individual child read.

Miscue analysis seems to affect the way in which teachers approach their practice in a quite radical way. Because it involves looking at text and response on the three different linguistic levels, teachers find themselves thinking and talking about language itself quite differently. They argue with each other about the coding of, for example, substitutions, and become consciously aware of the constraints of written language. They say that once having used miscue analysis, they internalise its approach, and never listen to a child read in the same way again.

When recall is added to the analysis, they see that there are many discrepancies between apparent fluency in oral reading and real understanding. They notice that, even more puzzlingly, a child may stumble in reading aloud and yet recall with accuracy and insight. The problem-solving nature of reading and the complexities of the process are highlighted.

So the influence on teachers' attitudes is probably greater than any immediate action taken as a result of analysing one child's miscues. In the long run, this less obvious influence of miscue analysis may cause great change in the primary classroom.

The fundamental interest of Kenneth Goodman and the psycholinguists in miscue analysis is in the extent to which children bring sense to their reading. His overall question is 'Do the miscues affect the meaning of the whole passage?' Bettelheim and Zelan (1982) take a different tack, and ascribe oral reading errors to deeper causes, arising from subconscious feelings. Negative mistakes, they say, arise from boredom with banal material. Controversially, they explore substitutions psycho-analytically, giving examples of cases where children make deviant responses, not because they do not know the original words, but because they do not *want* to say them. For example, they describe a child reading the following passage from 'Black Beauty':

> Then someone ran to our master's house and came back with a gun; presently there was a loud bang and a dreadful shriek, and then all was still; the black horse moved no more.

The girl read 'deadful' for 'dreadful'. Asked what had happened, she answered: 'The horse was shot because it had a broken leg.' 'Since the horse was shot', we replied, 'its shriek certainly was deadful.' In reaction to this, she looked at the text and said 'Oh, no, it says "dreadful".' (p. 166).

Bettelheim and Zelan suggest that the child's feeling for the event and for language was so strong that she was able to invent a new word spontaneously.

This approach may seem far-fetched, and there is a danger of reading too much of significance into oral reading errors. It does however underline what is now generally accepted, that motivation and attitudes – the affective dimension – are as important, if not more so, than intellectual aspects in learning to read.

Miscue analysis, therefore, gives insight into a variety of strategies, and is most valuable for helping teachers to become aware of the complexities of the reading process. Where we have probably not exploited it sufficiently as yet is in bringing children – the readers themselves – into ensuing discussions. There are possibilities for encouraging pupils to listen to their own reading on tape, and to discuss what is going on, with the aims of helping them toward cognitive clarity and the expression of their feelings about the text. It is debatable how far young readers should be automatising the reading skill, or attempting to think about it as a conscious act. To the extent that we isolate and concentrate on phonic rules we seem to encourage only awareness of the surface features of written language. It seems to be just as important to show the child what is happening when he or she makes an 'informed' contextual guess in reading.

One of the less direct influences of miscue analysis, therefore, is that 'listening to reading' becomes a shared enterprise rather than an asymmetrical tester-testee situation. If responses are triggered by all sorts of psychological factors, it is interesting and rewarding to find out more about these by discussion. Margaret Meek and a group of teachers (Meek, 1983) made a longitudinal study of the interaction between themselves and older backward readers, and came to the conclusion that the greatest progress was made when the teachers managed to pass the 'initiative for learning' over to the pupils, despite the fact that they were self-confirmed 'failures'. They proposed that more open-ended questioning and more pupil talk were vital in reading acquisition. They realised that the activity could not be subsumed into a set of procedures which would be valid in every case – 'the rationale for the teaching of reading is always in evolution for the teacher.' (p. 222)

The elicitation of free recall after oral reading supports their suggestions, as it gives fascinating insights into the thought processes of the readers. The art of expanding limited recall by asking leading, open-ended questions is a subtle one. The teacher must be careful not to impose his or her own framework of response on what has been read. As older children begin to make fewer mistakes on the surface level, their ability to tap levels of meaning becomes the most important element in their reading. Two responses to the passage below (approximately 11 year reading level) are worth discussing in this context.

The Sportsman (Arnold, 1984)

I know that if you are going to be really good at sport you have to concentrate on it completely and give up all your spare time and energy to it. At seven years old I determined to be a great footballer. I thought I had the right build for it, and my footwork at that age was pretty neat. I practised so hard that several windows of the house were broken, and my ball was confiscated for a week, which broke the concentration as well as the window.

By the time I was ten, swimming had become my main occupation, and I spent most of my time butter-flying across the pool, swallowing large gulps of water in my excitement. Unfortunately I dived in one day without realising that the pool had been emptied (I am short-sighted), and although my head turned out to be harder than the pool bottom, it seemed to dampen my enthusiasm for the sport.

At twelve, I acquired a snooker table, and became cross-eyed as I perfected my strokes. The shock of finding out, when I finally persuaded a partner to play with me, that I was colour-blind, put paid to my dreams of a misspent youth.

I have now discovered how to be really good at sports without any exertion at all. I sit in front of the television and impress my girl-friend by pointing out all the faults of the players; it is much more comfortable and less dangerous than participation, and my girl-friend thinks I am wonderful.

MICHAEL (chronological age 9.3)

Michael: It's about sportsman and when he was seven he was a good football player and then when I was about ten or eleven I went swimming and then when I was about eleven I dived in without any – um – with no water in the pool so I got eye-sighted and then, when I was about fourteen it was I played snooker and I had to do the strokes really good because I was eye-sighted.

Teacher: But weren't you something else as well? No? Go on, tell me about how you finished off then.

Michael: And then my girl-friend said I was wonderful.

Teacher: Why? What did you decide to do in the end? Did you become a sportsman eventually?

Michael: Yes.

Teacher: Did you?

Michael: Yes.

JEREMY (chronological age 8.8)

Jeremy: A sportsman – you have to be good at things, a football player you have to be good at passing and good at things. Playing snooker you have to be good at your shots and pot the ball –

Teacher: Try to tell about the story you have read. Who was the person in the story.

Jeremy: The person who was talking in the story was trying things out and playing things. Trying all the things he could do – looking up how to do them.

Teacher: What else? What did he find out in the end?

Jeremy: He found he was going colour-blind and cross-eyed so he tried to –

Teacher: What sports did he try?

Jeremy: Tried swimming, football, he tried snooker and eventually he got a partner for snooker. He found his best sport was – he tried to watch sports and tell people about them.

Teacher: And who did he tell?

Jeremy: He told his girl-friend about them and all the faults they had made.

Teacher: So did he actually become a sportsman?

Jeremy: No, he didn't become a sportsman.

Teacher: So the story really tells us what?

Jeremy: What he was doing to try to become a sportsman.

Teacher: But he didn't?

Jeremy: He didn't.

It is interesting to trace the different ways in which these children attempt to synthesise the text, both of them with a basis of good oral reading. We can detect how much further the second boy has gone in overall grasp and in sticking to his convictions about what he has read – and in his desire to bring his own generalisations about sport into the dialogue. Incidentally, all the children who read this passage were confused about the nature of colour-blindness and short-sightedness. More importantly, none of them spontaneously reflected the irony or the exaggerations of the passage in their recall. Only through such discussions can we begin to probe the ways in which a satisfying and total response gradually emerges.

Parental co-operation

The necessity for longer periods with individual readers has begun to affect the organisation of reading in the classroom; the teacher finds that he or she needs more time. This may have partly contributed to the next important influence which has been brought to bear on hearing children read – the move towards parental involvement.

Whereas in the past teachers held on to the professionalism of hearing children read as their specialist preserve, they have now realised that perhaps their professionalism lies elsewhere. Many ventures have been documented since the 'Belfield Experiment' was described by Peter Wilby in the *Sunday Times* (29 March 1981, p. 33). Parents have in some cases been asked to take over the practice of hearing their children read almost exclusively, either at home or in school. This has often resulted in the parents themselves becoming more interested in reading, and in their becoming more aware of the problem-solving nature of the process. It has had the bonus of freeing teachers to concentrate on functional reading. The partnership has been almost entirely fruitful. In a useful publication from the Reading Centre at Reading University, Root (1983) describes the response to an article she had written in *Child Education*. Forty schools responded, all praising parental involvement. Most of the schools welcomed parents hearing children read, from once or twice weekly to nightly. The co-operation was often reinforced by discussion and carefully constructed advice sheets. 'Parent help allows for more reading aloud time and liberates the teacher to do more diagnostic work.' (Root, 1983) Root's book describes how parents' attitudes, initially influenced mainly by their own memories of school learning (for example, insistence on repetition of a book till learned, over-emphasis on word accuracy), changed radically.

Reading schemes

Another aspect of parental involvement leads to consideration of the last influence on change in listening to children read. Many parents who began to work with their children complained that the basic schemes they brought home to read were inane, and they subsequently began to share in the choice of books within the classroom. The practice of hearing children read has invariably been closely linked with the universal use of basic reading schemes. Miscue analysis has made teachers aware of the paucity of language of many of the early readers, and the near-impossibility of utilising the syntactic and semantic cueing systems with 'Up, Janet, up!' or 'Can Nan fan a pan?' The desire to get away from an extrinsically motivated mastery of skill at the expense of meaning has led them to question the necessity of graded readers. Freer schemes which incorporate well-written children's literature (Cliff Moon's Kaleidoscope packs (1981), for instance), have shown that the prop of carefully-controlled vocabulary is illusory. The use of schemes has led to an over-emphasis on the skill of decoding words. The text is usually artificial and detached from children's experience of spoken language, since readability criteria are based on frequent repetition of words, short sentences, and a very limited vocabulary. Bettelheim and Zelan (1982) demonstrate how vocabulary load in readers has actually diminished across the years: First readers in the 1920s contained on average 645 different words; in the 1930s 460, in the 1940s and 1950s 350 words. Between 1960 and 1963 pre-primers ranged from 54 to 83; primers from 113 to 173. Some teachers, even in infant classes, report that the rejection of schemes and learning to read through real books has been completely successful.

Communicative reading aloud

Although the purposes for hearing children read are beginning to be more clearly thought out, the use of reading aloud for communicative purposes has probably decreased. Individualised learning/teaching methods have led, in some schools, to children working silently on their own throughout the day. Valuable opportunities for sharing reading experiences are not therefore exploited. Initiating situations involving reading aloud to others merits consideration, especially as the tape-recorder gives opportunity for storing what has been read for transmission at an appropriate time. The usual sequence of reading aloud in order to progress to silent reading is in this case reversed – children select and prepare, as a result of silent reading, to read aloud to others. Opportunities for oral reading arise naturally in the course of the day; for instance, in the activity of group prediction amongst a small group, each with a copy of the same book. When the group comes together to discuss what might happen in the ensuing chapter, they return to the words of the text to support their evidence. If a group is asked, for example, to select what they think are the most exciting, or the saddest, or the most mysterious passages, they will willingly read and re-read in order to make a programme of those passages for the rest of the class, or for younger children.

Hearing children read will change radically in the future, because of the influences described. They are already beginning to affect the pattern of organisation in the classroom. 'The school should seek not to make primary reading the fetish that is has been. The reading should always be for the intrinsic interest or value of what is read . . . it should never be thought of as an exercise.'

This is not an exhortation by a modern radical, but words written by E. B. Huey in 1908!

Some conclusions

In summary, the future pattern will probably include the following ingredients:

1 recognition that oral reading and silent reading should proceed simultaneously, from entry into school;
2 longer periods given to individual reading interviews, which will necessitate re-organisation of the curriculum, with a greater emphasis on group work based on collaborative learning;

3 the group work will have clear outcomes, many of which will start with silent reading and result in reading aloud for communication;
4 the teaching of phonics will be seen as one possible cueing system only, resulting in the use of more intrinsically interesting texts which will enable contextual hypotheses;
5 the realisation that books as such may be diminishing, will demand that other forms of print are incorporated into reading aloud in school, for example, from computers and tele-text;
6 the teacher's professionalism will be accepted as lying in the understanding of the reading process and the development of the child, and in his or her power to train the child to read independently for real purposes as early as possible.

References

Arnold, H. (1982) *Listening to Children Reading* (UKRA Monograph). Hodder & Stoughton.

Arnold, H. (1984) *Making Sense of It: Graded Materials for Miscue Analysis*. Hodder & Stoughton.

Bettelheim, B. and Zelan, K. (1982) *On Learning to Read*. Thames & Hudson.

Biemiller, A. (1970) 'The development of the use of graphic and contextual information as children learn to read', *Reading Research Quarterly*, 6, 75-96.

Boydell, D. (1978) *The Primary Teacher in Action*. Open Books.

Campbell, R. (1981) 'An approach to analysing teacher verbal moves in hearing children read', *Journal of Research in Reading*, 4, 43-56.

Francis, H. (1982) *Learning to Read*. Unwin Educational.

Goodman, K. (1969) 'Analysis of oral reading miscues: applied psycholinguistics', *Reading Research Quarterly*, 5, 9-30.

Gulliver, J. (1979) 'Teachers' assumptions in listening to reading', *Language for Learning*, 1, 42-56.

Meek, M. (1983) *Achieving Literacy*. Routledge & Kegan Paul.

Moon, C. (1981) *Kaleidoscopes*. Books for Students.

Potter, F. (1980) 'Miscue analysis: a cautionary note', *Journal of Research in Reading*, 3, 116-28.

Root, B. (1983) *Parents in Partnership.* Centre for the Teaching of Reading. University of Reading.

Smith, F. (1971) *Understanding Reading.* Holt, Rinehart & Winston.

Southgate V., Arnold, H. and Johnson, S. (1981) *Extending Beginning Reading.* Heinemann Educational for the Schools Council.

Spencer, M. (1981) *Report on Conference on Investigating Talk* (Schools Council Language for Learning Project). London Institute of Education.

7

Information skills through project work

David Wray

We live in an age of information and an age in which the ability to deal with information relevant to one's purposes is becoming increasingly vital. It is therefore extremely important that such a vital ability should at least begin to be taught during the school years. The evidence, however, would suggest that in general schools either make little attempt to develop this ability in their pupils, or if they do, it is done very ineffectively. This is a sweeping assertion, and naturally there are some glowing exceptions to this, but the growing recent interest in the teaching of information skills, whether under the title of study skills or of library-user skills, is indicative of a realisation of both a need and a weakness in much present educational practice. This chapter will attempt to analyse some of the possibilities for the teaching of information skills in the primary school curriculum. It will do this through focusing on one particular area of teaching common to many primary schools: that of project or topic work.

In recent years evidence has begun to accumulate that the learning opportunities which project or topic work presents are rarely exploited to the full. What commonly seems to happen is that project work comes to consist of the accumulation of large amounts of haphazard information, often copied directly from reference books. This can often result in very presentable end-products but, when questioned, the children may have little or no idea of what they have learned in the process. This chapter will attempt to determine some of the reasons for this state of affairs and then will go on to suggest ways in which teachers can overcome these problems.

Some reasons for ineffective project work

There seem to be two basic reasons for the ineffectiveness of much project work. The first may simply be that pupils have not mastered the skills necessary to pursue effective project work. The very sophisticated nature of these skills should not be underestimated.

> We award the highest academic accolade to a student who can see a question, focus it into an enquiry, trace sources, find relevant information in those sources, collate the information, reorganise that information in a way that meets the question posed, and write up the reorganised material as a report. To those who achieve that pinnacle of scholarship we award a Ph.D. This same process is the one we have adopted as the main teaching method for the less academic and less well-motivated school pupil . . . Yet we often give no specific help (Marland, 1977)

Marland's comments about secondary school use of project work surely apply even more forcefully to the primary school.

A second likely reason for the ineffectiveness of project work is that the activity itself does not have a clearly defined purpose on the part of either the teacher or the pupil. Teachers may do project work for reasons more concerned with class management than skill development, and the use of project work as a means of advancing skills may not be exploited. Certainly, if one were to divide the primary school day up into 'skills and frills' sections, as it often is by teachers and others, then it is highly likely that project work would come in the 'frills' section. How often is project work, for teachers, put on a par with art and craft, or games: that is, something to be done after the major work of the school day, basic skill work, is finished?

For pupils also the purpose may be undefined. They may approach the task with very little precise notion of what they wish to achieve. How often is their only guidance a vague wish to 'find out' about something, be it dinosaurs, railways or whatever? Rarely will they define precisely what it is they wish to find out about dinosaurs or railways, etc.

Deficiencies in this area have been summed up by Maxwell in his review of junior-school reading in Scottish schools.

Though the majority of teachers reported grading reading requirements according to pupils' abilities, the general practice did not include close supervision of pupils' reading, and it appeared that frequently the interested and able pupils read widely on a topic while the poorest readers did little other than copy short statements or cut out pictures. Some teachers gave ad hoc help to pupils in the use of reference books, but there appeared little systematic guidance given to pupils on the reading and study techniques required to make the most effective use of their time and efforts. (Maxwell, 1977).

The general picture, then, is of project work being rather a vague area, with little attempt being made to capitalise on its potential as a teaching technique.

Some possibilities for project work

The reader may be forgiven for thinking at this stage that, given the weaknesses in much project work, the solution would be to abandon it altogether. However, that would surely be a great pity, because project work should have a great deal to offer as a means of developing reading and other skills. Its greatest asset lies perhaps in the motivation it can engender amongst children. If children are allowed and encouraged to work in areas which interest them, this ought to be a useful means of demonstrating to them the usefulness of developing their reading skills. There is some evidence that children perform at a higher level in their reading when they are really interested in what they are reading about (Belloni and Jongsma, 1978), and project work would seem an ideal area in which this could happen.

It ought also to be useful because it provides a context which is meaningful to children, and in which a variety of reading skills can be learned. With regard to such skills as those involved in finding information in books and libraries, it has to be asked, where else in the curriculum apart from in some kind of investigatory work can these skills be acquired and practised? It would certainly not seem sensible to teach these skills in a context which did not allow children to put them to use immediately, nor would it seem sensible to teach them through sets of exercises independent of any meaningful content area. It is possibly this kind of teaching which is most likely to lead to situations such as those found in the Nottingham reading study (Lunzer and Gardner, 1979), where secondary-school children could explain how to use a contents page or an index perfectly well, but when observed in their work, did not actually use these things much at all.

> Most of the children . . . had a verbal knowledge of how to select a book and how to find what they wanted in the right book once they had located it. Almost certainly, the knowledge was inadequate. They could not use it in real life . . . We conclude that children need help and guidance in a real context to convert the verbal knowledge to behavioural competence.

Project work at the very least can provide that 'real context' in which children can see the point of learning skills such as using an index, because these skills can make their work easier. Such a situation would also seem a very sensible place to teach these skills, given the twin assets of high motivation to learn, and the immediate practice of skills as they are taught.

Improving project work

If it is agreed that project work has a great deal to offer in terms of developing reading, but recognised that these opportunities tend not to be exploited to the full, it is necessary to examine ways in which project work can be designed to make fuller use of its potential.

There seem to be two major criteria which are crucial in carrying this out. Project work needs to become purposeful rather than vague, and systematic rather than haphazard. To make it purposeful one of the first steps is to define carefully what children are expected to get out of this work. From a teacher's point of view, one of the main things they should gain is a development in specific skills connected with finding and using information. What children gain in terms of content is surely of secondary importance. After all, teachers are not generally too concerned with whether a child learns exactly what the average length of a brontosaurus was, or exactly how wide apart railway lines are, but they should be concerned that the child has the skills necessary to find out that information should it be required.

The argument is thus that the major purpose behind project work from a teacher's point of view should be skill development rather than knowledge acquisition. The nature of these skills will be discussed below, but at this point it is necessary to recognise that seeing the process in this light may create a gap between a teacher's purpose and a child's purpose for engaging in project-work methods. From the children's point of view, what they really want to get out of a project is precisely the content which, for teachers, has just been relegated to a secondary position. It is the content of a project which gets children interested, quite naturally, not the fact that they may develop their reading skills. This idea is for the child an abstraction which is difficult to appreciate. There is thus a clash of interests between teacher and pupils. The important thing seems to be that teachers should be aware of this conflict and take some steps to resolve it, and this involves some kind of negotiation between teacher and pupils. Teachers need not be afraid of explaining to pupils *their* reasons for wanting them to carry out a certain piece of investigatory work. The work should be planned carefully, however, to ensure that the pupils are getting something out of it as well. The concept of negotiation would seem fairly central to the planning of effective projects.

The second criterion put forward earlier was that project work should be systematic rather than haphazard. There seem to be two major ways of looking at this. One is to be systematic from the point of view of the skills it is aimed to develop through this kind of work, which involves a close definition of the skills necessary to complete a project satisfactorily, and then to structure the work to include the practice and development of these skills. The second is to look at the process used for introducing and developing projects in the classroom and ensuring that this follows a well-defined plan. These two points of view seem important enough to discuss in much greater depth.

Defining project skills

The first task then is to define the skills which children will need to complete a project effectively. There have been a number of analyses of this nature put forward. One analysis which has proved useful is to look at the issue as a process of dealing with information, and to define the skills involved in this process as information skills (Winkworth, 1977). This analysis produces six distinct stages, as follows.

Define subject and purpose

The first stage involves a clear definition of the subject of the enquiry and the purpose for it. The need here is to encourage children to be precise about what they want to find out in their work. A vague purpose, such as 'I want to find out about dinosaurs', is not precise enough to be useful, and has two logical consequences. First, children have no way of judging the relevance of any information they do find. Presumably any information about dinosaurs is equally relevant.

Second, there is no indication of when the process of finding information should stop. Children could go on for ever finding out information about dinosaurs and be no nearer satisfying this vague purpose. They clearly need some assistance from teachers to become much more precise in defining their areas of enquiry. In this case, a more precise purpose might be, 'I want to find out the relative sizes of the most common dinosaurs so I can draw scale pictures of them on a wall chart.' This defines the area and clearly specifies what they are going to do with the information once they have found it.

Defining precise purposes in this way clearly involves some degree of prior background knowledge on the child's part. A general familiarising time spent browsing through encyclopaedias, or other general resources, may be an important phase of a successful project. After this, however, the child will need to spend time in consultation with the teacher and classmates, defining precise areas for subsequent investigation.

Locate information

The second stage is that of actually finding the information in whatever sources are appropriate. This naturally includes the skills of using a library, such as dealing with catalogues, the Dewey system and swiftly locating the books needed on the shelf. It also includes the skills of using books, such as using the contents and the index to track down the topics required. The use of specific reference tools such as encyclopaedias and atlases would also come in here. At this stage, too, the use of the more modern tools of information technology will be of increasing importance. Using Prestel, Ceefax and other technological information systems demands a new set of location skills. Children will clearly need to be taught all these things and, as the Bullock report points out (DES, 1975), there ought to be little difficulty in teaching these things if, and it is a big if, they are taught in a practical manner so that children can see that they do actually help them. The Nottingham finding (Lunzer and Gardner, 1979) is again relevant; children who could explain how to use an index did not generally of their own accord actually use one very often. They clearly did not see it as very useful to them.

One way around this problem should be to teach these skills in a practical way, in a context in which the children themselves can see their usefulness. A project in which the children's desire to acquire information will engender high motivation would seem a far more appropriate way of achieving this than putting them through special library lessons, divorced from any meaningful context. The efficiency of books of exercises with pages entitled 'Using an index', or 'Using cross-references' would seem very dubious.

Select information

At the next stage of the process, having located the information they require, the children reach what is probably the most difficult part: that is, lifting the information off the page in some meaningful fashion. The evidence suggests (Maxwell, 1977; DES 1975, 1978) that what happens at this stage is very often simply copying. Some possible reasons for this have already been mentioned. One may be that children do not have sufficient command of the skills of extracting information from a text. In other words their comprehension is at fault, or put another way the text they are using is too difficult for them.

Another reason may be, again, that they have very little precise notion of what they want to get from a particular text. One way of improving this situation is to encourage them to formulate specific questions to which they wish to find answers. These questions need not simply be factual, they can also be interpretive. For example, they might want to know why a particular event took place. The point is that they are unlikely to find answers to these questions neatly encapsulated in a few words, and so they are forced to be selective in what they read. This is where the skills of skimming a text to gain a general impression, and scanning to glean specific points, are very useful, and it is at this point within the process of finding information that they would perhaps most effectively be taught.

If children have specific questions to answer, then their reading is given a clear purpose, and purposeful reading is presumably the aim of all teaching of reading. Within a project, there is a strong chance that the questions the children have are questions which are intrinsically important to them, rather than questions the teacher has imposed upon them, for whatever reason. There is also the possibility that the high motivation to acquire information that project work ideally involves may be sufficient to overcome problems due to text difficulty, or poor comprehension ability.

Organise information

The fourth stage of the process concerns what they do with the information once they have found it. Skills such as note-taking come in at this stage, and one way of approaching this is to use the questions originally formulated as a structure for notes taken, so that children are noting down things they need to know, rather than every conceivably useful point. Using pre-formulated questions as a structure for notes also provides more able children with a useful means of synthesising information from a range of sources. Again, this should reduce direct copying to a minimum. Also, at this stage, the compiling of a bibliography can be very useful. Even very young children can get into the habit of jotting down the sources of their information as they go along. This not only enables them easily to recheck particular information if they need to, but it also has the effect of encouraging them to consult a wider range of sources of information. How often do children expect to find all the information they need from just one book? Searching through a variety of sources will give them a wider perspective on their study area, and may also give them contradictory evidence. This will force them to progress to the fifth stage of the information process.

Evaluate information

The children then have to evaluate the information they have, and they should be able to use a variety of criteria to judge the truth, relevance and status of the information they find. This might seem rather beyond primary schoolchildren, but Zimet (1976) has shown conclusively the need for all children to become aware of possible bias, intentional or otherwise, in the books they read. In a project, this could perhaps involve examining texts such as the different accounts of the events leading up to the Norman Conquest by Anglo-Saxon and Norman contemporary writers. A simple clash of information will be found if books published ten years ago dealing with modern technology (computers, etc.) are compared with those published since 1980. There are also many texts which can be used in the primary classroom which intentionally present a one-sided view. Advertising material is an obvious example. Children need to know what to do in these cases if they are to get at the truth, and they also need to be shown that print is not necessarily infallible. A questioning attitude towards books and other printed texts would seem an important one to develop in young readers.

Another thing children need to do in evaluating information is to ask themselves 'How does this information fit with what I already know?' It does seem fairly common for children to produce project work consisting entirely of reiterations of knowledge they already have, rather than advancements of that knowledge. This, of course, satisfies neither the teacher's nor the child's aims. As previously argued, beautiful end-products are not in themselves sufficient justification for project work. Some learning must surely also take place.

Communicate results

In the final stage of the process, the children need to decide on some way of presenting their results. How they do this depends on three things: their initial purpose, their potential audience, and the nature of the information they have.

They may have intended to present the information as a factual account, or they may have been investigating a particular area with a view to using the material obtained as a background for a piece of more imaginative writing. This latter technique can be very useful, especially in historical projects. After all, to write a sensible story about, say, a Viking voyage, involves considerable background knowledge, and this has to be obtained from somewhere.

With regard to the audience for children's project work, it is becoming widely agreed that it is important for children to learn to take into account their potential audience when they are producing written work. Writing for children in other schools might be a useful way of developing the ability to do this, and certainly many schools have found this 'experience-exchange' a very valuable means of increasing children's motivation to improve both the content and the presentation of their writing.

Finally, the information found may lend itself to various forms of presentation, ranging from fact sheets to some kind of argument for or against various issues. There may also be

possibilities for some kind of diagrammatic representation of
selected information.

An approach to teaching

Having established the skills aimed at in project work, a
possible systematic way of approaching them in the classroom will now be discussed. This is based unashamedly on a
system which will be familiar to students of Open University
reading courses. There may, obviously, be other equally valid
ways of approaching this.

The system divides a piece of project work into four basic
stages. At first, teachers will have to go through these stages
quite carefully with the children, but eventually it is hoped
that the children will become independent enough to use the
system, or one like it, by themselves.

The four stages are:

1   Goals – determining goals or aims;
2   Plans – making plans to achieve these goals;
3   Implementation – carrying out the plans;
4   Development – evaluating success, and using this
    evaluation to review goals and plans for next time.

This system will now be applied to project work in the
classroom.

Goals

The children decide what they want to achieve in their work.
They work out a purpose, and decide on what they are going
to produce, what form it will take, and who will be the
intended audience. Naturally, at least to begin with, the
children will not be able to do this all for themselves, and the
goal-setting will take place in collaboration with the teacher.
Both children and teacher will suggest ideas and together they

will work out and *negotiate* a set of goals. The teacher's main function in this negotiation is most likely to be to encourage the children to become more precise in their setting of goals: that is, to take them gradually beyond the vague 'find out about' stage.

Plans

At the planning stage again there will be negotiation between teacher and children and they will together work out how they are going to achieve their goals. What activities will they need to be involved in? What resources will they need? Where will they get them from? What will they do with them when they find them? What organisational factors need to be taken into account, such as space for working, time, the numbers of children involved at any one time, and how they can make sure nothing important is missed out?

These kind of decisions are normally made by the teacher alone, but it is possible that involving the children in making them might be an extremely effective way of teaching them self-determination and discipline. They might also come up with some ideas the teacher had not thought of.

Implementation

It seems particularly important that at the implementation phase the children are not simply left to get on with it. This can, in fact, be the most productive teaching time, because the children will be involved in very real problems and their skills will be being rigorously tested. It ought to be possible for the teacher at this stage to spot skill weaknesses, and to introduce activities designed to remedy them – activities of which the children can see the point. For example, if teachers notice that a child or group of children are tending to look for information in books simply by leafing through them, hoping to find the information by accident, they can, at this stage, point out the use of the contents and index pages, and run through some quick games using these. For instance, 'Who can be the first to tell me which chapter is about dinosaur eggs?' and so on. These activities in themselves are no different from the kind of activities often found in books of exercises, but here the context is crucially different. The children are not being asked to do the exercises as a matter of course, when they cannot really see the point. They are not in this vacuum-like context. They are being engaged in activities which have a direct relevance to work they are already involved in, and which *they* can see are designed to help them do this work more effectively. As previously argued, this sets skill development activities firmly within a context in which the children can see the importance of mastering these particular skills, simply because they can make the children's work towards their goals significantly easier.

Development

The final stage of this process is sometimes referred to as the evaluation stage. However, the title development is useful because it highlights the fact that something has to be done with evaluations: something to improve the process next time around.

Fairly naturally, when a project is completed, and indeed while it is still in progress, the teacher will be giving hints as to how it might be improved, and making evaluations. This is after all a major part of a teacher's role. It is necessary to consider, however, to what extent teachers can develop within their children the ability to evaluate their own progress and achievement in a project. In the world outside school there will not always be a teacher around to point out weaknesses and suggest improvements in children's information-handling.

Children can be encouraged to look back at how they found particular pieces of information and to ask themselves whether this was done in the most efficient way. They can also be asked to test out their finished product by investigating whether it in fact does the job intended. It was suggested earlier that one of the goals to be decided for any project was the intended readership of the final product; that is, its audience. After a project is completed, children can pass on their finished product to its intended audience, which may be classmates, or children younger or older than themselves, or even adults in or out of school, and can then evaluate the audience's reaction.

For example, one very valuable potential audience for project work might be younger children in the same school. Fourth-year juniors can produce project booklets for first or second-year juniors. A good test of the suitability of the material they choose, and especially its intelligibility, is whether these younger children can read and understand it, and find it enjoyable. Naturally, the best way of finding this out is to ask them.

The need for a school policy

So far, project work has been considered in terms of what an individual teacher can do with his or her class of children. However, as with every part of the curriculum, there is a wider perspective to be taken into account, and that is the fact that there is a limit on what an individual teacher can achieve if he or she is not working in harmony with the rest of the school. It clearly needs to be a part of the school's work on developing its curriculum to consider the place of project work within this curriculum, and to plan ways in which it can be utilised to maximum advantage, especially as a vehicle for the teaching of information skills. There is, then, yet a third way of being systematic with regard to project work, and that is for a school to work out a definite policy on how it should be approached and which particular skills should be stressed at which levels. If this is done, then the work of individual teachers within the school contributes to the general pattern of pupils' development, rather than being wasted because it is not adequately prepared for, or followed up by other teachers. Of course, how this policy might be arrived at is an issue in its own right and takes us into the field of school-focused inservice work and curriculum development.

Conclusion

This chapter has tried to suggest that the poor image project work seems to have as a teaching method is not a necessary one, and that there are strategies which teachers and schools can employ to ensure that it becomes purposeful and systematic. There can be little doubt that its potential is very great, as it provides the opportunity for effective teaching of skills of finding and using information within a context of high pupil interest. This unique combination is of too great a value to be wasted.

Note

Much fuller discussion of the points made in this chapter, together with many practical suggestions for developing project work, will be found in Wray (1985).

References

Belloni, L. and Jongsma, E. (1978) 'The effects of interest on reading comprehension of low-achieving students', *Journal of Reading*, 22, 106-9.

DES (1975) *A Language For Life* (The bullock report). HMSO.

DES (1978) *Primary Education in England: A survey by HM Inspectors of Schools.* HMSO.

Lunzer, E. and Gardner, K. (1979) *The Effective Use of Reading.* Heinemann.

Marland, M. (1977) *Language Across The Curriculum.* Heinemann.

Maxwell, J. (1977) *Reading Progress from 8 to 15.* NFER.

Winkworth, F. (1977) *User Education in Schools.* British Library R. and D. report 5391 HC.

Wray, D. (1985) *Teaching Information Skills through Project Work.* Hodder & Stoughton.

Zimet, S. (1976) *Print and Prejudice.* Hodder & Stoughton.

8

The microcomputer revolution in reading

David Williams

REMark: introduction

Ten years ago, a computer was a large, static and very expensive piece of machinery, operated by an expert elite who communicated with it in a language which only they understood. Today, computers are small, portable and cheap, and may be programmed by schoolchildren with an ease and assurance that terrifies their parents.

These developments have inevitably set in motion yet another of those educational bandwagons which most teachers have by now learned to view with extreme caution. Surely the microcomputer will go the way of all such gimmicks, that is, embraced with enthusiasm by teachers if not by pupils, only to prove more revolutionary in theory than practice? Its usefulness overstated, its flexibility limited, it may even increase teacher workload, despite claims to the contrary. Excitement fades to disillusionment, and so another piece of technology goes to gather dust on a storeroom shelf.

This time, however, the sceptics are wrong. In the next decade, microcomputers will stimulate radical changes in every part of the educational system. Their potential has already been recognised and exploited in other fields – schools will not so much be moving with the times as running to catch up. Ideally, the reading courses of the 1990s will not only look different to today's teachers, they will be unrecognisable.

READ: what can the microcomputer do now?

The programs available at present fall into four main categories, as outlined below.

Data: the electronic worksheet

These are learning programs that don't pretend to be anything else. Austin and Lutterodt (1982) describe these as programs 'that permit self paced and individualised instruction with the benefit of a wide range of graphic aids'. The screen becomes an individualised blackboard for each child. Ideally individual children should be able to move through the program at their own speed, and if a page is not understood they can be moved to a subroutine that explains and reinforces the point of difficulty, then tests their understanding before they return to the main program. If groups of children use the program then a great deal of peer-group tutoring goes on, though supervision is needed to prevent the brighter child moving on before they all understand.

To be effective, the programmer must have a clear objective, and be able to predict areas of difficulty and provide subroutines to deal with them. It is essential, therefore, that an experienced teacher of reading is directly involved at all stages of programming.

A successful program of this type is no more than a computerisation of traditional classroom method, and it will teach most children effectively, with the added advantages of constant individual attention and limitless patience. (The role of the teacher in the classroom is to deal with all the problems that the computer cannot solve – helping the child who *still* doesn't understand, hearing children read, and acting as manager, counsellor and troubleshooter.)

Example 1: cloze. The computer presents a cloze passage on the screen. The deletions may be chosen either by the teacher or the computer. The child types in a guess for each deletion in turn. After each one, the computer compares the guess with the answer in its memory. If they match, the answer appears on the screen – if not, the child is asked to try again. It is essential that the child spells accurately – if the match is not exact, the answer is rejected. Alternatively, the answers may be listed at the side of the screen for the child to select from. It is possible to have more than one acceptable answer for each deletion.

This process can be fairly sterile done individually, but it really comes to life when pairs or groups of children discuss the possible answers.

The advantage of using the computer is that the answers are confirmed immediately rather than after the whole passage has been completed.

Example 2: mixed up sentences. The computer presents a jumbled sentence on the screen, e.g. 'John school went bike on his to'. Below the words is a picture of a boy, a bike and his school.

The child must type the sentence with the words in the correct order, and is rewarded for the right answer by the picture coming to life – John jumps on his bike and cycles to school. Once again, accurate typing is essential as the computer will not respond to misspelled words. It is possible to allow the child to move the existing words about the screen by means of a light pen, cursor control or joystick, but requiring him or her to type them in encourages correct spelling and concentration.

Example 3: event sequencing. A number of sentences that describe a sequence of events are presented on the screen in random order. The child decides on the correct order and types a number against each sentence. The right answer is rewarded by some animation. If the answer is wrong, the child is asked to try again. For example:

John's Day

Sentence	Graphics
1 John gets up	Stick figure in bed then standing by bed
2 John gets dressed	Clothes appear on stick figure
3 John eats breakfast	food on breakfast table disappears
4 John gets the bus to school	Stick figure leaves house, waits at bus stop, is collected by bus
5 He plays football in the yard	Stick boys play football

Example 4: parts of speech. The computer asks children to type in five nouns, five verbs and five adjectives. It then prints a story using these words, usually highlighting them in colour. Children really enjoy this exercise – for a time! They put in their own names, and chuckle over the story. Most programs of this type have several stories in memory. Of course it is important that the child should know what these parts of speech are!

The children quickly learn that the computer cannot discriminate between noun, verb, adjective or preposition and will happily use whatever is typed in. The computer accepts wrongly-spelled words, nonsense words and rude words and displays them on screen in the story to the amusement of the class. Supervision is needed!

Example 5: writing a story. More imaginative programs are being written. In one, the child is invited to write a story with the computer, choosing from a list of possible scenes. Supposing the child selects 'Football match'. The screen clears and a green pitch appears. The computer asks 'What would you see at a football match?' The child thinks/discusses with partner and types in 'police'. The computer scans its memory, finds 'police' and prints little blue policemen around the perimeter of the pitch. Gradually the picture is built up. If the child cannot complete it, then he or she can ask the computer to help. The computer could offer suggestions, e.g. 'There are eleven ____ in a team', or might produce a list of words containing one the child hasn't tried. The child spots it, types it in, and if the picture is complete, a whistle blows (computers can produce sounds!), and a player runs with the ball and scores a goal.

The computer asks the child if he or she wants to work the section again or choose another scene. The scenes can be connected with a piece of animation. If the child chooses 'The Farm', the screen would show a figure leaving the football ground, getting on a bus, and travelling off the screen. A countryside picture would appear, the bus would arrive, stop, the figure would alight, and the process start again.

Data: learning can be fun!

Many word-games already used in classrooms are extremely effective on the computer. Children enjoy the challenge of trying to beat the machine, and the screen display makes the game more interesting. The insistent demands of the computer make it hard for attention to wander, and unlike a human opponent, it cannot be sidetracked, or exhausted.

The word-games reinforce spelling and reading skills, and encourage accuracy.

Example 1: a popular word-game. The object of the game, to construct small words from a long word, is made more interesting by the use of graphics. The computer prints a word, e.g. caterpillar, with a picture of a long green caterpillar beside it. If the child types in 'pill' the caterpillar will move down the screen, pick up the word, move up again, and place it in a list of correct answers. An incorrect word will produce the instruction to 'try again'.

The computer totals the number of responses and the

correct answers; then when the child can supply no more words a full list of all possible words will be displayed, with the child's answers in colour.

Example 2: hangman. The program memory will contain a long list of words that will tax the resources of most children. It is usually possible for the teacher to type in a list of words so that the game can be aimed at a specific child, providing additional experience of words that may be giving difficulty.

The child types in the letter choice. The letter disappears from the alphabet printed on the screen and reappears in the hidden word, if correct. If the letter is wrong, then the scaffold begins to build!

There may be some temptation for the child to fail deliberately in order to see the man hang, now that many computers have high resolution graphics! A reviewer of a hangman program recently suggested that the detail was so gruesome as to be unsuitable for young children!

Example 3: wordsearch. There is a program available that will automatically create wordsearch squares from a list of words supplied by teacher or pupil. The puzzle can be left on screen and the child then uses a light pen or joystick to indicate the hidden words. (The letters would change colour.) If a printer is available then the puzzle on screen could be dumped to the printer and the wordsearch would be solved in the usual way.

Example 4: scrabble. There is a commercial program aimed at adults which has a library of 10,000 words, and can play against several players at once. It will query a word not in its memory, but will accept it if a player asserts that it exists. There are four different levels of play, and reviewers claim that the fourth is almost unbeatable. It will even suggest a word if the opponent is stuck!

In junior Scrabble, the children either fill in words already on the Scrabble board, or select words from a list. This makes an ideal classroom game, since it focuses on words, demands concentration, and children enjoy it.

A computerised version would have a number of levels based on key words, e.g. high-frequency spellings, and also enable teachers to introduce new vocabulary. Children would be able to compete both with each other and the machine. The satisfaction in beating the computer is phenomenal!

Data: goblins in the classroom – adventure games

The children control a character who is embroiled in a perilous adventure. This character (we will call him Samson) may have a set of attributes such as wisdom, strength, dexterity and charisma, that determine his chances of success in a variety of nailbiting situations.

Samson traditionally starts his adventure in a dungeon, tavern, cave, castle, haunted house, Transylvanian mansion, top security establishment, huge spaceship, wilderness, hobbit hole, or, unusually, a quiet English village. There will be an objective for Samson to attain before the game is won. This may simply be treasure and dead monsters, but is more likely to involve a search for a magical object or group of objects that have been carefully guarded and hidden. The children's objective is to make sure that Samson survives, builds up experience and gathers items that will help him in his quest, and eventually enable him to complete his mission. The adventure will become increasingly complex, deadly and demanding as it progresses. Building up experience and discovering magic items gives Samson an enhanced chance of surviving the later stages of the adventure.

These games involve a lot of reading. Most of them come with explanatory booklets detailing the words and commands the computer understands, and include a description of each cave or room that Samson might enter. The adventures usually contain puzzles that have to be solved, cryptic advice, plays on words, red herrings, and some really useful information that is only revealed when you've asked the computer the right question, correctly phrased.

Adventure games are complex. Children on an adventure will need to make decisions quickly, interrogate the game's database, read the instruction book carefully, compare clues with known facts, weigh evidence and plan strategies.

Unless the reading teacher has a microcomputer at home with a lot of memory, he or she is unlikely to have seen an adventure game. At present they are commercial rather than educational. I hope that the following simulation of a small part of a dungeon adventure will make reading teachers aware of the potential of this type of game. You will note that the language used is not always syntactically correct. The computer understands exactly the same by 'Get sword. Kill dragon' as it does by 'Get the finely engraved sword and kill the horrible green dragon'. Children become aware of this and tend to communicate in only those words that the computer understands.

The adventure game is time-consuming. A short adventure may take several hours to complete, and that doesn't count the times your character was killed and you had to start again. Happily, some adventure games save the state of the game to tape so it can be continued at some other convenient time. The adventure ties up a computer for quite a long time. At present, with relatively few computers in schools this will be a problem, but hopefully in the future there will be plenty of computer time available. With one-and-a-half to two million microcomputers in British homes, many children are already playing adventure games at home.

Game simulation

Situation: Room 101 is 20 ft square, rough hewn out of solid rock. There is a heavy wooden door in the East wall. There are two chairs and a small cupboard in the South West corner of the room. Some rusty weapons are stacked in the North East corner.

Samson has just killed two goblins whom he surprised in the room.

Computer: What are you going to do?
Child: Search South wall.
Computer: You find nothing.
(The computer doesn't always reveal the whereabouts of traps, secret doors and invisible creatures the first time of asking, unless Samson has high intelligence or is experienced.)
Child: Search floor.
Computer: You find nothing.
Child: Search table.
Computer: You find 20 silver pieces. (Computer increments Samson's treasure total.)
Child: Examine weapons.
Computer: Treasure No. 6. (Referring to booklet, child reads that Treasure 6 is a rusty sword with runes inscribed on the blade.)
(Quite clearly this is a magic sword. The child will discover from experience whether the sword glows in the presence of evil, does extra damage to the undead, or perhaps is a cursed sword that makes it easier for monsters to find and wound Samson.)
Child: Pick up sword. (Computer adds it to list of treasures discovered so far.)
(Searching and examining take time. There is a good chance of being disturbed by a wandering monster the longer Samson remains in a particular location.)
Child: Go to East door. (Often the room plan appears on screen and Samson can be moved within the room.)
Child: Listen.
Computer: Footsteps. (If you are experienced and intelligent and listen again, the computer may reveal the type of creatures that are approaching.)

At this point the children have to make a decision. Stay and fight, or run away? Is Samson's strength rating high enough to withstand injury? Is he tired from his hectic battle with the goblins? Indeed, is there any point in an unnecessary fight with the monsters that are approaching the East door?

    Child: Go to North door.
    Computer: Three goblins come through East door. Are you going to attack, retreat or use magic?
    Child: Open door. (If you're going to retreat, the door must be open. If you try to go through a closed door you may injure yourself!)
    Computer: (Door opens on room plan.)
(The goblins move towards Samson.)

Furious discussion amongst the children. What to do next? If three giants had come through the door there would have been no choice but to retreat. Three goblins are an entirely different matter. They can be disposed of easily, whilst their weapons stand little chance of piercing the adventurer's plate armour.

    Child: Fire.
(Some adventures allow you to attack a specific target, e.g. 'attack goblin 2': you may have attacking options. You can use a sword for close fighting (comands such as thrust, swing and parry), a bow for long distance work, and you may have the option of magical attacks too!)

In some games the fighting is described in detail and the children are under pressure to make decisions. If they are slow to decide what to do, the goblins may get the chance of an extra hit!

    Computer: You fire an arrow. (This can be seen on screen.) It hits goblin 2. Goblin 2 falls to the ground, dead. Goblins 1 and 3 attack you. (A moment of tension passes.) They miss.
    Child: S(wing). (As you fight you become tired. If you are heavily laden with treasure you

might only manage a couple of swings of the sword before you have to rest, during which time your opponent can batter away at you!)

Computer: You swing your sword. You wound goblin 1. Goblins 1 and 3 attack you. Goblin 1 strikes your head. (You notice that Samson's wounds score has suddenly changed from 100 per cent to 60 per cent. It's time to retreat. Unfortunately your two attacks have left Samson very tired and he hasn't enough energy to move. You decide to try a magical attack which doesn't consume normal energy.)

Child: Use staff. (Samson found this rune encrusted item at the start of the dungeon. You know it's a magical item and hope he can use it.)

Computer: A lightning bolt kills goblins 1 and 3. You've won!

(The computer adds the value of the three goblins to Samson's experience point total.)

The children now have several decisions to make. Is Samson strong enough to continue exploring? Perhaps it would be better if he retraced his footsteps and left the dungeon with his treasure, then tries again when he has recovered his full strength. If he continues exploring, he may bump into something really nasty and die. On the other hand, there is a fair chance that he might find a magic potion which will restore him to full strength and heal his wounds.

Data: simulations

Another type of game that involves a lot of reading, and where the child is required to process large amounts of information, take decisions on the basis of that information, and see the consequences, is the simulation. Some simula-

F

tions, such as flight, are largely nonverbal, but some have a high verbal content. One such is the football management program, and there are several different versions of this for different computers.

The child has to type in the name of his or her team and the squad of players, and identify the best players. There is lots of scope for discussion of the merits of local footballers, decision-making and accurate spelling. Then the interaction starts.

> Computer: Your first round match is at Wimbledon. Wimbledon are top of Division 3. Their home record is W 10, D2, L 0. Goals for 24, against 7.

(In some programs it is possible to discover more about your opponents by using the 'scout' function.)

> Child: Scout. (The computer doesn't always give extra information.)
> Computer: Wimbledon play 4–2–4. They shadow opponents in defence and play a short passing game in attack. They take corners to the far post and have a direct shot at goal from a free kick.

On the basis of the information given the children will discuss their tactics for the match and decide the instructions to be typed in. Paper and pencils will be needed.

Once the tactics have been carefully typed in, the match starts. The game can be entirely verbal, or a mixture of words and graphics. Teachers of reading will prefer games that give a running commentary. Children get very excited when the match is in progress:

> Newcastle kick off
> Keegan passes to Waddell on the wing
> Waddell cuts inside the Wimbledon No 4
> Waddell chips the ball towards goal
> The goalkeeper catches the ball and throws it to the Wimbledon No 3

No 3 passes to No 6 who dummies McDermott
No 6 fires a shot at goal
Thomas saves brilliantly
Thomas kicks the ball upfield to Waddell
Waddell passes to McDermott
McDermott hits a pass to Keegan
Keegan fires a shot at goal
The Wimbledon keeper fumbles the ball
Waddell gets possession and hits the ball into the
back of the net
It's a goal!!
Wimbledon 0 Newcastle 1, after 7 minutes play

It may take five minutes of real time to play the match. At half time you can change your tactics and bring on a substitute. A key player might be injured and have to be replaced.

The speed that the commentary scrolls up the screen can be controlled from the keyboard on some computers. If the program is written in BASIC it is a comparatively easy matter to insert an instruction to hold print on the screen until it has been read by the children.

If we continued with the program you would notice that a lot of the phrases are repeated. e.g. passes to, cuts inside the, chips the ball towards goal, the goalkeeper catches the ball and throws it to, who dummies, fires a shot at goal, saves, brilliantly, kicks the ball upfield to, and so on. The number of phrases that can be used is only limited by the computer's memory.

This type of program would really score with poor reading football-mad boys. They would begin by laboriously inputting lots of names and instructions. They could use speed control to read each line before the next comes up. They wouldn't need to use speed control for long because most phrases and names are frequently repeated. As their reading speed increases, so does the excitement! The spin-offs in written work are considerable. Each match could be reported, headlines written for newspaper sports pages, records kept of results and goal scores, league tables compiled and updated after each set of matches.

Most of the games on the market would be more popular with boys, e.g. football, or science fiction adventure, and little effort has been made to provide games of more general interest. Other sports would make good computer programs, e.g. lawn tennis, show jumping, or team athletics, as well as simulations of jobs such as managing a pop group or running a boutique.

A game that would challenge both boys and girls is organising a household budget. The child would be allowed a sum of money to feed a family for a week. The computer has in its memory a list of foods and prices. The child decides on the meals and buys the food. The object of the game is to avoid starvation!

Simulations are a good way of getting children reading painlessly in a real-life situation.

Other uses

Stephen J. Clamp (1983) suggests that 'teaching computer awareness and simple programming skills is a useful addition to the curriculum.' I would go further and assert that typing simple programs into the computer is a useful spelling and reading experience. Most computer magazines publish short games programs. Reading and spelling accuracy is encouraged as the child copies one of these program listings. If a mistake is made then the program won't 'run'. 'Syntax error' or some other error message will appear on the screen and the child will have to find and correct the mistake. The reward for accuracy and good concentration is a program that works and that the child and his or her friends can play.

David Wray (1983) describes another program type which should be of great interest to the reading teacher. The program involves the interrogation of a computer database for information. For example, a crime might have been committed and the child have to question witnesses. The computer plays the part of witnesses and criminal. The child must phrase questions with care, compare and record answers, sift evidence and deduce the identity of the criminal. This could be an individual activity but, as in many verbal computer games, group play is preferable. As David Wray (1983) asserts, 'Major benefits will be in the discussion and decision making processes involved.'

Several additional uses for the computer are described by George E. Mason (1983): using the computer to administer diagnostic tests; letting the child teach the computer; and using the computer as a 'focus for student hostility'(!). He describes a program called ELIZA which enables the child to hold a coherent conversation with the computer. The computer recognises some of the words and phrases which the child types in and reflects them back at the child as open-ended questions that encourage the child to reply.

As with other verbal games the child must type in the sentences correctly spelled and has to read the replies which, for the most part, will be in standard English. At first it is easy to believe that the child is engaged in an equal dialogue with a machine intelligence, so apposite are some of the replies. After a time, most adults will realise that the apparent intelligence is clever programming: the child may not!

Computers used as word processors are appearing in offices, colleges and universities. Simple word-processing programs often used in conjunction with microwriters are already being experimented on in a few schools. Children type their stories into the computer or microwriter. They can insert, delete, correct, paragraph, title, and move chunks of text from place to place. When the child is satisfied with the text, the story is printed. Another refinement might be to use a disc-based 'spelling checker', which highlights words in the text that the computer cannot find in its vocabulary of 40–50,000 words. The finished text will, in appearance, be of a professional standard with all that that implies for the child's image of him or herself as a writer.

END: conclusion

Computer-based individualised reading programs will benefit
all children once there are enough computers in our schools.
The poorer readers will benefit most of all. Ainscow and
Tweddle (1979) state the problem: 'Slow learners often
develop a poor opinion of themselves, lose confidence and
bring an expectation of failure with them into the classroom.'
The same is true of all children whose level of literacy is low.
Once behind their peers they need individual attention to
improve their reading. The computer can provide this
attention.

The computer:

1 always offers an encouraging, positive response;
2 provides a successful experience;
3 lets the child work at his or her own level;
4 treats the child as an individual;
5 gives instant feedback which is essential for correcting
  bad habits;
6 presents reading in a peer-approved way;
7 is highly motivating.

One day, the primary teacher guiding children through
their instructional computer program may be able to prevent
reading failure altogether. Until then, the computer will be of
considerable help to the less successful reader.

The pace of technological change is quickening. Once the
laser-read optical memory discs are widespread, it will be
possible to computerise entire reading schemes. Schools will
be able to buy a reading scheme which will take all their
children from non-reader to fluent reader with the computer
directing and providing the child's learning activities. In
addition, the computer would run reading and diagnostic
tests, offer remedial programmes and keep complete records
of child attainment. Child reading profiles, detailing work

done, books read, skills learned, spellings known and test scores, would be printed by the computer in a few seconds.

However there are dangers. Reading has schools of thought. A reading scheme could, for example, be produced by those experts who see reading as being based on a hierarchy of skills. Any process with a clearly defined end and intermediate objectives that can be broken down into easily analysed subskills is ideally suited for computerisation. Teachers will have to judge whether computer schemes meet the needs of children, but also what scope there is for teacher initiative, knowledge and intuition once the scheme is in operation.

The microcomputer revolution has begun. Teachers of reading need to keep a firm hold of their hats, their expertise and their integrity. They must play a major part in developing, using and controlling the new technology, not for their own benefit, but for the sake of the children they teach.

References

Ainscow, M. and Tweddle, D.A. (1979) *Preventing Classroom Failure.* Wiley.

Austin, G.R. and Lutterodt, S.A. (1982) 'The computer at school', *Prospects* (UNESCO), *12*, 421-38.

Clamp, S.J. (1983) 'Computer assisted learning and the less able', *Remedial Education, 18*, No. 1, 15-18.

Mason, G.E. (1983) 'The computer in the reading clinic', *The Reading Teacher, 36*, 504-7.

Wray, D. (1983) 'Computer assisted learning in language and reading', *Reading, 17*, No. 1, 31-6.

9

Classroom-based assessment

Peter Brinton

In recent years teachers have been increasingly called upon to make more use of classroom-based assessment techniques. This has been very forcefully put by HMI in the recent Primary Survey (DES, 1978): 'It is vital that teachers should be knowledgeable in what they teach. It is just as necessary that they should be able to assess the performance of their pupils in terms of what they next need to be taught' (para 8.58). What is true of primary education must surely be true of all sectors of the educational system.

This chapter explores some of the techniques currently available to the teacher, setting them in a clear philosophy of what the reading process entails; it also calls for a general renegotiation of the contract between the teacher and the taught, particularly in the area of assessment. The links between the ideas and methods contained in this chapter and those by David Wray, Colin Harrison and Helen Arnold are obvious. Project work, Wray argues, provides the meaningful context in which classroom assessment must take place. The readability of the text is of paramount importance when considering its appropriateness for use with a group of children. Helen Arnold's work on hearing children read is an example of a specific type of classroom assessment. Since her own chapter describes her work in detail, it will not be considered in the following discussion.

The reading process

Reading is a psycholinguistic process. It is more than the passive act of receiving and processing the graphic symbols from a printed page. It is rather an interaction between each reader (including all their previous experiences, biases, etc., and their purposes for reading the text), and the text itself. The reader is continually striving for meaning from what he or she reads, and filtering that meaning via past experience (See Smith, 1978; also, DES, 1975, 6.1-6.6). Mention must also be made of the range of texts that the reader has to cope with – prose, time-tables, official reports, newspaper reports, advertisements – as these will affect the approach the reader takes on each occasion. Additionally, in the context of this chapter, reading is more broadly seen as including the planning of work, the use of assessing skills and the production of a finished written article where this is appropriate.

Standardised and informal assessment

There are three reasons why it is necessary to test children. First, it is sometimes useful to relate ability to some national average, with a view to gauging how an individual, class or school fits into the national pattern. Second, a test may have a diagnostic element which will highlight any strengths or weaknesses children have. Third, testing can inform the next stage of the teaching process. This is where the essential difference between standardised testing and informal assessment occurs. Standardised testing generally provides the teacher with only a single score or quotient on which to base any evaluation of the child's ability. Informal assessment, if it is to have any worth in the classroom, should provide much more than this, because its basis lies in the materials which the child is using daily.

Where standardised tests do have a diagnostic element and provide more than just a single rating of ability (the Richmond Achievement Tests and the Edinburgh Reading Tests being examples) there is a danger of teaching to that test. This is contrary to the advice of the inspectorate and its calls for a broader base to the curriculum. Another danger in standardised testing in the classroom context is that a test only covering one facet of reading behaviour can, if care is not taken, be interpreted as a general indicator of ability. The most glaring example of this must be the frequent abuse of the Burt word-recognition test, which is too often taken as a general measure of reading ability. The use of limited measures may label children without any meaningful basis for the labels. Statistical concepts such as *validity, reliability* and *norms* play a prominent role in standardised testing and these too are important in informal assessment.

Validity refers to the extent to which the test serves the purpose for which it was intended. For example, if a test is intended to assess the child's word-recognition ability, does it do this job and include no other factors?

Reliability is a measure of consistency. Reliability can take many forms. It can be a factor related to time: if a child is tested on day one and re-tested on day five, would the scores be similar? It can be a factor related to the tester: would the child's score have been similar if teacher B had administered the test rather than teacher A? It can be a factor of test items; would the child's score have been similar if 'equivalent' testing items had been used for the assessment?

Norms refer to typical performances for clearly defined reference groups. The most common norms refer to age groups. Is the score or quotient on a test at, above or below what has been found typical for that age group? When examining standardised tests it is important to check when the norms were constructed as typical performances vary with time, and what might have been a typical performance 20 years ago could well not be typical today.

How do these three statistical concepts relate to informal

assessment? First, norms have no real role to play because generally one is only comparing an individual with previously accepted criteria of competence or with their past performances. Reliability and validity are important, however. Reliability strongly relates to sampling. How often must one assess or observe an individual to judge their competence or otherwise? Also, in how many contexts must this assessment take place? There are no easy answers to these questions, but guidelines may be found in the following sections. Validity opens up a different series of questions. Are the judgements made about a child's ability sound? Here task analysis and structured observation have an important role to play because it is through these two related concepts that accurate assessments about what a child has to do to complete a task successfully can be made. Task analysis and structured observation are discussed in detail in later sections.

Informal assessment

There was much concern in the primary survey (DES, 1978) about 'match'. This means the appropriateness of material presented to individual children with regard to their ability and level of development. With standardised tests there is little opportunity to establish any 'match' between materials and child. Classroom-based assessment, however, provides abundant opportunities for such a consideration.

Liddell (1982) provides an alternative label for classroom-based assessment, *formative assessment*, which he describes as 'just good teaching'. Formative assessment is the teacher's attempt to evaluate how well pupils have coped with a particular skill, group of skills or body of knowledge within the curriculum, and as a result of that to lead them to improve those areas to the best of their ability. There are a wide range of methods available to the teacher to enable this process to take place and these will be discussed in turn later; however, firstly, it is important to examine what might be termed the basis for informal or classroom-based assessment.

The basis of classroom-based assessment

The philosophy of classroom-based assessment is that children should be given the opportunity to demonstrate their abilities on 'normal classroom activities', and that this leads to the next teaching input. This means that the focus of interest transfers from 'the test' (and ensuring its correct administration) to the child. The child is now being provided with situations in which to demonstrate his or her abilities, but the threat of 'testing' is removed, and a context for the child's assessment is gained.

So that this assessment through normal classroom activities can take place, however, it is necessary to examine the activities, first from the child's point of view, and then from the teacher's point of view, to see what the content of each activity is. How the child and the teacher perceive each task is central in terms of what they will both eventually learn from it.

Teachers see the work which they present to children at two related levels. First, they see the skills a child needs to complete each task set, and, second, they see the facts and ideas in which those skills are embedded. Unless there is an element of content, there can be no process of working on that content and thus no development of skills. However, children generally view the learning process only from the standpoint of the content, the facts and ideas. Interest, enthusiasm and need should be their prime motivators to complete a task.

Task analysis

Kerr (1981) suggests that when designing materials for their pupils, teachers do not work from 'precisely designed objectives, through lesson design and materials selection to instruction and evaluation'.

He continues by quoting MacDonald who states that

teachers 'rarely ask "What am I going to accomplish?" Instead teachers try to determine "What am I going to do?"' This view is supported by Zahorik (in Kerr, 1981) who concluded that teachers did not begin with objectives but with a consideration of the learning activity – in other words, of its content.

Given that this is how many teachers operate, then the analysis of reading tasks put forward by Fyfe and Mitchell (1981) would seem to be appropriate.

For two reasons they prefer not to base their analysis of materials presented to children on an analysis of reading skills. First, they point to the lack of consensus on the nature of the reading process and question whether or not it *can* actually be itemised into skills. Second, they agree with Kerr (1981) in believing that teachers often develop their work around themes and develop reading within these contexts. Fyfe and Mitchell, then, see reading in terms of tasks and classify these tasks into five main areas: (a) search; (b) comprehend; (c) personal response; (d) learn or store; (e) do. They state that these five elements are not discrete and that the majority of tasks will demand a combination of several of them, though they cite comprehension as the major element.

Task analysis, then, can be seen in terms of the teacher looking at the activity the child has to work on and arriving at conclusions on the sort of decisions a child will have to make to complete that activity. Here, however, despite Fyfe and Mitchell's reservations about a skills analysis, it can be argued that such an analysis should take place. In the initial move to give this type of assessment greater prominence, teachers may benefit from a more detailed study of this kind. However, as the process becomes part of their professional make-up, less intense analysis may suffice.

Methods of informal assessment

Before looking at a variety of methods of informal assessment, we must consider a few general points. The function of this section is not to provide formats for use, but rather to look at the strengths and weaknesses of the different approaches. The selection of the most appropriate methods for a wide variety of occasions, and the devising of formats to fit the teacher's, children's and school's needs, depends upon the individual teacher's professional judgement.

Structured observation

Whatever the method of presentation the teacher decides to adopt in any particular circumstance, at the very root of classroom assessment must come an evaluation of the educational worth of the materials and skills presented to the child.

One method for doing this is structured observation. Here the teacher looks closely at how the children are coping with any particular task and assesses their strengths and weaknesses on that task. With regard to materials, the teacher's approach must be to evaluate those materials in terms of the children's written or spoken response, and judge whether each child's response shows a real and relevant understanding of the problem set. Two very useful aids in this area are packs presented by the Open University's Centre for Continuing Education. The two packs, P533 – *Curriculum in Action: An Approach to Evaluation* (published in 1980) and P531 – *Purposeful Learning: Reading and Language* (available shortly), concentrate on these two aspects.

P533 – *Curriculum in Action* bases its approach around six basic questions:

1 What did the pupils actually do?
2 What were they learning?
3 How worthwhile was it?
4 What did I do?
5 What did I learn?
6 What do I intend to do now?

A major criticism of this approach could be that any analysis might be superficial, with participants merely confirming their own prejudices. For this reason it is probably better for teachers to study packs of this nature as a group, with the collective wisdom of the group being applied to each individual's responses.

P531 – *Purposeful Learning: Reading and Language* looks at the related problem of the type of material presented to the child and his or her response to it. It is this child's eye view (or rather, the attempt to get a child's eye view) that gives this particular pack its strength. Any mismatch between text and response can be evaluated in terms of understanding, textual complexity, information-collection and the use of that information. Again, a major problem could be one of superficiality and the expectation of a stereotyped response. If the pack is worked through by a group of teachers, with a person of experience taking the chair, then the problem may be alleviated.

Marking

It would be easy to forget or gloss over this most common and regular method of informal assessment. Marking has too often consisted of placing a score or grade at the end of a piece of work, or at best a written comment. If marking is to be effective it must lead the pupil to produce another, more polished, draft of that particular piece of work or to improve the quality of the next piece of work.

Liddell (1982) suggests six points that teachers should consider when responding to children's writing:

1 assessment should occur as close as possible to the time of writing;
2 bear in mind the pupil's previous level of performance;
3 take account of the original purposes for the writing;
4 be selective;

5 identify only what the pupil is felt capable of improving;
6 point the pupil towards the means of improvement.

He considers that the teacher's primary task is to try to understand the pupil's ideas, no matter how muddled these might be, and to display this understanding through praise; not empty praise, but praise which shows insight. If the teacher respects the pupil's ideas, so will the pupil. However, this is not the end of the process. The pupils must be directed to see where their meaning is not clear so that they can begin to sort out the problem themselves. This leads on to the skill of proof-reading. If pupils can be encouraged to look critically at their own work, then they can begin to correct their own errors.

Implicit in this approach is the notion of redrafting of work to lead to an improvement in both content and style. This could be carried out by the pupil in isolation, but a more interesting notion is that of the 'editorial board'. Here small groups could critically examine each other's work and suggest refinements and improvements at the structural, grammatical and lexical levels. On occasions the 'final draft' could be 'published' in some kind of class magazine or the like.

Criterion referenced testing

A method of assessment that follows directly from the task analysis approach is criterion-referenced testing. In criterion-referenced testing, success or otherwise is not based on any reference to the performance of others (norms) but to the individual's ability to meet some previously-defined criteria of competency. It is through task analysis that these criteria can be established.

The model for a criterion-referenced approach usually takes the following form:

State the task → Teach the task → Test the task

It is usual for the criteria for success to be stated in behavioural terms (i.e. what the child actually has to do), as this makes the testing and the evaluation of the results much more straightforward.

This method of assessment can be useful when the teacher wishes to ascertain the level of competence of a particular child or group of children after either a new skill has been taught or a new set of facts and ideas has been introduced. One of its great strengths is that because there is no reference to the performance of others, greater account can be taken of different levels of ability. A level of success can be decided upon for individual children and their performance judged against that level. Its validity comes from the task analysis which precedes the teaching of the task and its reliability comes from the testing of the task in the final stage. However, to ensure greater reliability, the testing or assessment should take place in a variety of contexts. If the child displays a similar performance in a variety of contexts, then the performances can be taken to be an accurate assessment of the child's learning in that particular area.

Cloze procedure

Knowledge and use of cloze procedure must be widespread in the classrooms of the British Isles. It involves words being deleted from a text and being replaced by blank spaces of equal length. The text deletions can be drawn up either on the basis that every nth word is deleted or that words are deleted on a grammatical basis (i.e. verbs, conjunctions, etc., are deleted). Harrison (1980) suggests that if deletions are being made on a structural basis (every nth word), then every fifth word is the minimum possible because below that level the contextual information needed to fill in the blanks is too small. Every seventh word is generally thought to be the optimum deletion rate.

When the cloze text has been prepared, the child then reads

the passage and fills in the blanks, responding to both the semantic and syntactic clues contained in the writing. It is usual to give a short 'lead in' of a few sentences without deletions to set the scene for the reader. To ensure reliability, about 50 deletions are needed in any one passage. This has the added advantage of making percentage scores easier to work out.

Depending on the use to which the results are going to be put, either the originally deleted word or one which serves the same function can be considered appropriate. An example of when the originally deleted word could be used as an indicator of success is placement of a child in a fiction-reading programme or aiding a decision to move the child within that programme. This use is based around the accumulation of research which indicates that if a child gets 75 per cent of the deletions correct they are reading at an instructional level (i.e. need some help from the teacher), and that with over 90 per cent of the deletions correct they are operating at an independent level. A system could be set up whereby a school has a bank of cloze texts at a variety of reading and interest levels and pupils can be tested on these where necessary.

An example of where it may not be appropriate to use the actually deleted word is when cloze procedure is used in small groups. Small groups of children could be provided with copies of a cloze text and asked to discuss among themselves which words they would choose to fill in the gaps. If the ensuing discussion is then tape-recorded the reasons and justifications for the insertions can then be analysed by the teacher. This view is supported by Harrison (1980), who quotes both Walker and Lunzer and Gardner in suggesting that this method encourages children to consider the text as a whole and not just to operate at the 'word' level.

In recent years, the educational catalogues have abounded with pre-packaged examples of cloze passages, group prediction and sequencing exercises. The temptation for teachers is to use them in the same manner as English grammar exercises were once used. The underlying theme of this discussion has been that classroom assessment must be assessment in context, and that context should be the project and thematic work carried out by the children, where their motivation is high and they have meaningful and purposeful tasks to perform. It follows, therefore, that if any assessment by cloze procedure, group prediction and group sequencing is to be made it must be made with this relationship in mind.

Informal reading inventories (IRIs)

Generally, IRIs have concentrated on the analysis of oral reading. This is borne out by critical reviews (Pikulski, 1978) and practical examples (see Senior in Raggett, Tutt and Raggett, 1979). Part of the example given by Senior is as follows:

My house

<pre>
                          ch
h   br   cl   d
My house has a red roof and a brown chimney. The door and the
                                              h-a
          with   question mark c-au cave
windows are blue. ~~Will~~ you come and play with me? We can have
      b-u   sh-kip
    s-u-b-   wi-ll   s-k
cake and buns to eat. We will run and skip and jump in the garden
         s-it   r-e-st
then we will sit down and rest.
</pre>

The purpose of this example is to show the type of format involved rather than to analyse the reading strategies used by the child. As can be seen, the teacher's copy of the text is typed out with spaces for the child's oral miscues to be recorded. From an analysis of the miscues, a programme of reading instruction can be formulated. IRIs are the forerunners of miscue analysis. However, with the crystallisation of miscue analysis into a workable classroom system (Arnold, 1982), the use of IRIs for this purpose would appear to have diminished. This should not be a reason to abandon IRIs but a spur to extend their use into other areas such as planning project work, goal-setting, identification of bias and the evaluation of the finished product. The IRI would then become an annotated check-list, providing information about how a child approached the overall task of reading for some previously defined purpose.

When constructing this type of check-list four points need to be considered:

1 the level of difficulty of the task undertaken;
2 the level of proficiency achieved by the child;
3 a record of the increasing level of ability demonstrated by the child on the tasks;
4 an indication of the variety of contexts in which the task can be applied.

An example of such a check-list is shown in figure 9.1.

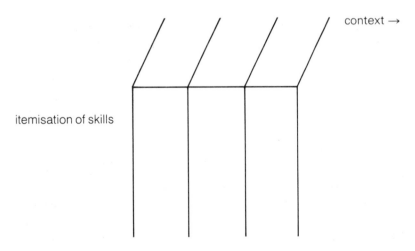

Blank – no degree of proficiency
/ – skill introduced
X – proficient in limited contexts
■ – proficient in a variety of contexts

Figure 9.1 Check-list

Group prediction and group sequencing

These techniques can be used to assess pupils' global understanding of texts or as an evaluation of the degree of coherent understanding each pupil is gaining from printed material. Group prediction involves children working in small groups. They are presented with the introduction to a story and invited to discuss what might follow. Then they are presented with the next extract. They can modify their prediction in the light of the new knowledge they have gained and continue to speculate on what might happen next. This process continues until the conclusion of the story. By using the increasing amounts of information contained within the text the children's predictions will, one hopes, become increasingly accurate.

Sequencing involves the slicing up of a text or set of instructions; the individual or small group has to replace them in the correct order. If possible, it is then a good idea to let the group carry out the task referred to in the instructions, as then they can be made aware, in a practical way, of their ability to find logic and order within a text.

As with cloze procedure these two activities are an assessment of a child's use of language beyond the word level. They have to identify the overall logic and coherence of the text and react to that. Group prediction, in particular, encourages children to make explicit the deductions they are formulating from the printed page, and to modify these in the light of increasing amounts of information.

However, this method of assessment, again, has its roots in classroom observation and unless this base has strong foundations in some type of task analysis then the conclusions drawn could have little substance.

Record-keeping

No form of assessment is worthwhile unless records of that assessment are kept. Without records, assessment is a sterile

business, existing in a vacuum. There are two basic questions
to be answered when devising a record-keeping system. Who
are the records for and how are they going to be kept?

In a Schools Council research study, Clift, Weiner and
Wilson (1981) questioned teachers on the function of school
records and highlighted seven major recommendations:

1 records should be a day-to-day record of teachers' work;
2 records should be a summary for internal school use;
3 school records should aid transition from school to
   school;
4 school records should aid transfers as well as transitions;
5 school records should have a diagnostic value;
6 school records should aid in problems concerning child
   welfare;
7 school records should aid the writing of reports to
   parents.

As this chapter is concerned with classroom based assessment, items 1), 2) and 5) are of prime importance, whereas the
other items stem from a consideration of these factors.

However, it is interesting to note that the teachers in the
survey also said what records should not be. It is worth
itemising these as a salutary reminder when devising any
record-keeping system. Records should not be:

1 a waste of time;
2 too jargonistic or lengthy;
3 used as a check on teachers' work;
4 a substitute for staffroom gossip (i.e. passing on prejudice);
5 a bureaucratic device for controlling pupils' lives.

Returning to the question of who the records are for, it
would appear essential that the majority of potential users of
those records should have a say both in their construction and
format. It is through involvement of this nature that their use
is more likely to be ensured. For example, if an infant school
is devising a system that may finally be used to aid transfer to

junior school, what better way to encourage the junior school to use those records than to invite them to help in the construction of the record-keeping system? This approach may have other long-term benefits, because records must reflect the basic philosophy and curriculum of any school. If they do not and the underlying philosophy of the curriculum the records are to reflect is not made clear, then to devise a record-keeping system would be akin to putting the cart before the horse.

In recommending guidelines for the construction of school records, Clift et al. split the task into two components: content and design.

Content

Content should:

1 be relevant to the purpose of the record;
2 be clearly sequenced;
3 give direct indications rather than implications for future teaching;
4 distinguish clearly between experience and attainment;
5 clearly present assessment information, stating:
    (a) the derivation of norms when grading or rating;
    (b) the criteria used when deciding on pupil competence;
    (c) details of standardised tests when rating or grading;
    (d) details of other testing techniques used;
    (e) teacher-made test marks in standardized form.

Design

Records should have:

1 a clear layout;
2 stable printing which will not fade;
3 clear section headings;
4 the pupil's name in a prominent position;

5 sufficient space for comments;
6 a prominently placed key.

All the above points have a major relevance to classroom-based assessment in two areas. First, if informal assessment is not to be idiosyncratic the criteria on which it is based must be made explicit and it must not dissolve into merely a chronological account of what any individual child has experienced. Second, they must complement and dovetail with any form of standardised testing the school and the local education authority wish to undertake.

Concise yet clear: these are the two important watchwords to keep in mind.

Summary

The aim of this chapter has been to look at classroom based assessment within a psycholinguistic model of the reading process. Several major points have emerged and these are stated below:

1 assessment should reflect the philosophy and content of the curriculum;
2 assessment should be based on a thorough understanding of the task a child is asked to complete;
3 assessment should be varied in both its forms and contexts;
4 assessment should be both reliable and valid;
5 assessment should aim to put the child at ease and hence elicit a 'best' performance;
6 assessment should show strengths as well as weaknesses;
7 assessment should inform the next stage of the teaching process;
8 assessment techniques should relate to the use to which the results are going to be put;
9 record-keeping should reflect both the curriculum and the assessment philosophy of the school.

References

Arnold, H. (1982) *Listening to Children Reading.* Hodder & Stoughton.

DES (1975) *A Language for Life* (The Bullock report). HMSO.

DES (1978) *Primary Education in England.* HMSO.

Clift, P.S. Weiner, G. and Wilson, E. (1981) *Record Keeping in Primary Schools.* Macmillan Educational.

Fyfe, R. and Mitchell, E. (1981) 'Formative assessment of reading', *Teaching English, 15,* 29-33.

Harrison, C. (1980) *Readability in the Classroom.* Cambridge University Press.

Kerr, S.T. (1981) 'How teachers design their materials: implications for instructional design', *Instructional Science, 10,* 363-78.

Liddell, G. (1982) 'The formative assessment of writing', *Teaching English, 15,* 4-10.

Open University. (1980) *Curriculum in Action – An Approach to Evaluation* (P533).

Open University. (in press) *Purposeful Learning: Reading and Language* (P531).

Pikulski, J. (1978) 'Informal reading inventories', in Chapman, J. L. and Czerniewska, P. (eds), *Reading: From Process to Practice.* Routledge & Kegan Paul.

Raggett, M. J., Tutt, C. and Raggett, P. (1979) *The Assessment and Testing of Reading.* Ward Lock Educational.

Smith, F. (1978) *Reading.* Cambridge University Press.

10

What's wrong with teaching reading?

John Merritt

In the United States there is a vast reading industry and a tremendously powerful reading Establishment. It is hardly surprising, therefore, that there is an ever-growing pressure on schools to buy expensive reading schemes and workshops for developing all aspects of reading at all levels from kindergarten through to university. In addition, an ever-increasing number of teachers enrol in programmes devoted to developing expertise in the teaching of reading. A similar pattern has been emerging in recent years in the United Kingdom.

Is this a hopeful sign? Does this mean that the Bullock report (DES, 1975) is at last bearing fruit? Can we look forward to a future in which every child will benefit from the ready availability of scientifically designed teaching material administered by a highly qualified expert? Or are we, perhaps, hitching our waggon to the wrong star?

It is, of course, quite reasonable to suppose that there would be a significant impact on reading standards if we devoted more money to resources for teaching reading, and to teacher training. It would be equally reasonable to suppose that the effects of such a policy on reading achievement should be obvious in any comparison between a country that devoted substantial resources to reading and one that allocated resources on a rather more frugal scale. On these grounds, a comparison could legitimately be made between reading standards in the United States and standards in the United Kingdom – particularly if the observations were made some years ago when the differences in our respective levels of provision for reading were even greater than at present.

Such a comparison of standards of reading in different countries throughout the world was in fact made in an international survey reported by Thorndike (1973). This survey showed, however, that the reading comprehension of American 10 year olds was appreciably less than that of children of the same age in Scotland and England – the very opposite of what might have been predicted. At the age of 14, scores for Scottish and American children were equal, with England falling into third place. It should be added that the greatest possible care was taken to ensure that the samples tested were as far as possible comparable.

On the question of training and qualification, Thorndike reported as follows: 'None of the variables showed a consistent relationship across the set of countries, though there was a slight indication that *membership in professional associations of educators or subject matter teachers* [my italics] was a favourable indicator' (p. 107). As to the availability of specialist teachers, the report says: 'There is no indication that children read better in schools with *many reading specialists even when the schools are equated for parental occupation* [My italics].'

The largest differences in reading achievement were in fact found, as might be expected, between countries with a relatively high level of economic development and a long tradition of universal education and countries much less well favoured in these respects. Within each of these two groups the differences were found to be relatively modest. Thus the overall level of education generally available seems to be as important as the allocation of special resources to reading.

On this evidence alone it would of course be somewhat facile to draw the conclusion that specially designed materials for teaching reading are of little or no value, or that special training in the teaching of reading is unnecessary. Nevertheless, the above findings do cast a considerable shadow over the current products of the reading industry and the kinds of training currently provided in the teaching of reading.

On the question of teacher training, most of us with responsibility in this area who studied the international survey probably saw these results as a criticism of courses run by other people! Naturally, we re-examined our own courses and even made quite substantial revisions. But we still felt that it would be ridiculous to assume that we could be on the wrong track altogether. Nevertheless, a severe critic could point to a study by Durkin in 1966 (see Durkin, 1974). She found that many children who read before starting school appeared to learn what they needed from older siblings. 'What', the critic might ask, 'does a specialist teacher of reading need to learn when a child can do the job without any such training?' The same critic might point to a study by Hassinger, cited in Corder (1971). Here high-school students with poor attendance records who were themselves retarded by two or three years in reading were used as tutors. After six weeks, the elementary school students showed a 4.6 months' gain and the high-school students who acted as tutors themselves showed a mean gain of eight months!

Naturally, we had our answer quite pat. Certainly, the unskilled youngster can teach reading as well as we can: almost anyone can – if they have only one child to deal with, or a fairly small group, and when they are close enough to the learning problem themselves to know what the learner's difficulties are. But we can't put 6 year olds or retarded high-school students in charge of classes of children. It seems reasonable to argue, therefore, that we do need to give teachers all the insights into the reading process, knowledge of strategies for teaching reading, and competence in any classroom management skills that may be necessary for coping with the wide range of reading ability to be found in a large class.

Before we go too far down that particular road, let us take into account a second major finding of the survey. In developed countries, it was found that home and family background provided

> an appreciable prediction of the reading achievement of individual students – and an even more substantial prediction of the average reading achievement of children in a school . . . When the population of a school comes from homes in which the parents are well educated, economically advantaged, and able to provide an environment in which reading materials and communication media are available, the school shows a generally superior level of reading achievement. (p. 177)

This finding is in line with most other observations of relationships between home background and educational achievement.

The relationship between socio-economic status and reading achievement is of course indirect. It just happens that the most active interest in a child's education is at present found among parents in certain income groups or occupational categories. But if this contribution could be boosted, a strong case could be made for a significant shift in the allocation of resources for reading in favour of programmes aimed at gaining substantial parental support.

In recent years, there has in fact been a steady increase in activities directed towards boosting parental support. Tizard, Schofield and Hewison (1982), for example, reported on an experiment in Haringey in which parents were encouraged to hear their children read each evening from books specified by the teacher. The children concerned gained more than those in the control group and more even than those who received extra help from a well-qualified teacher, and Hewison (1982) reported that the improvement was still apparent one year later.

Tizard, Schofield and Hewison (1982) drew attention to the inevitable methodological limitations which necessitated caution in interpreting their findings. Nevertheless, they were sufficiently confident to include the following among their conclusions.

1 In inner city, multiracial schools it is both feasible and practicable to involve nearly all parents in formal educational activities with infant and first-year junior school children, even if the parents are non-literate or largely non-English speaking.
2 Most parents express great satisfaction in being involved in this way by the schools, and teachers report that the children show an increased keenness for learning and are better behaved.
3 The teachers involved in the home collaboration also reported that they found the work with parents worthwhile and they continued to involve the parents with subsequent classes after the experiment was concluded.
4 The fact that some children read to parents who could not themselves read English, or in a few cases could not read at all, did not prevent improvement in the reading skills of those children, or detract from the willingness of the parent to collaborate with the school.

In view of the different kinds of evidence cited above one might well argue that we could, and should, as a matter of high priority, take full advantage of the wealth of resources already available – parents, the unemployed, and older children if we want to maximise reading achievement. They can do it. Why don't we give them a job? There are currently more parents readily available than there are teachers willing to use them. And there is a double benefit if we make use of parents in the classroom because what they learn from helping in the classroom can also be put to good use in the home. They also provide a pool of potential outreach workers to contact parents who cannot come in to the school on a regular basis but who might be pleased to participate in self-help groups of one kind or another. Thus, the best that we can provide by way of school experience can influence the home lives of our children and a great deal of what happens in the good home becomes practised as part of everyday classroom life.

Children currently in school can also both help, and benefit, in a similar way. It may be argued, furthermore, that the breaking-down of age barriers in schools for this and many other purposes is an essential element in educating children as responsible citizens and parents. Substantial training opportunities for learning how to handle this relatively new set of problems would obviously need to be provided both in initial and inservice courses.

This kind of development would affect all teachers in every kind of school. But then, the teaching of reading is, arguably, a responsibility that must be accepted by all teachers. Regrettably, although all teachers expect their pupils to learn from reading, the majority, if they are not teachers of infants or remedial specialists, assume that they themselves have no responsibility for helping their pupils to do so. If they do see a need, they assume that special periods set aside for developing effective reading provide the appropriate solution. Unfortunately, the skills learned in such contexts are far too limited, partly because of time restrictions, partly because of content and context restrictions, and partly because of the restricted perceptions of what is entailed in developing effective reading on the part of the teachers concerned. In addition, there is little or no inducement or opportunity for transfer of learning to occur outside the context of the reading lesson. Clearly, therefore, it is essential that *all* teachers be given appropriate training or experience in the teaching of reading.

All of this has significant implications for the nature and content of existing courses and inservice activities. Certainly, the idea that teachers need courses packed with linguistics and the esoterica of reading research seems increasingly hard to justify. Instead of asking, 'What else can we teach teachers about language and reading?' perhaps we should be asking,

'What knowledge, skills and insights will actually make any difference to their effectiveness as teachers within a community-orientated education system?' And having asked this question we need to be able to show that what we teach teachers actually does make a substantial contribution to professional judgement and is not merely a reflection of the political strength of the current academic in-group.

Even when a particular theoretical content is accepted as relevant we need to rethink its presentation and to decide what forms of learning will actually transfer to normal practice and result in more effective teaching. It is certainly at least arguable that a lot of what is currently included in courses could be presented in a very much simpler form without loss and that the conditions of learning in a great deal of initial and inservice education do not even begin to match those that we ourselves advocate in courses on pedagogy.

One of our present handicaps, I suspect, is that we tend in teacher training to start our analysis of what is needed in the wrong place. All too often we begin with a review of the kinds of theory which, we believe, can in some way or other add to a teacher's understanding of language in general and reading in particular. Unfortunately, such theoretical studies do not, in themselves, provide any guidance on priorities. They give no guidance concerning either the level of study or the amount of knowledge that might be optimal for generalists or for specialists, or for initial or inservice education. The result is that we either overload courses with theoretical content because we cannot justify leaving anything out, or we allow students to follow their own interests so that they are left with large gaps in their repertoire whose existence they may not even suspect or which, wrongly perhaps, they regard as trivial. In any case, competent practitioners do not start with a collection of theories and look for opportunities to apply them. They begin their analysis with the task to be carried out and then draw on whatever theory or theories are relevant. This, in itself, calls for a very different kind of course.

A further serious disadvantage is that any exploration of the possible range of significant relationships between different theoretical approaches is very time-consuming and rarely undertaken by those with a special interest in one kind of theory or another. Indeed, the exploration of significant relationships *between* theories of various kinds presents problems that are at least as complex as investigations *within* any particular body of theoretical knowledge. Teachers, however, like other practitioners, must be capable of drawing on a variety of theoretical considerations simultaneously. They are therefore at a serious disadvantage in courses at any level if the major emphasis is on the separate fields of study with only desultory and largely unsystematic forays being made to see how diverse theoretical considerations may be judiciously combined in tackling the range of practical problems that teachers need to cope with.

Another consequence of focusing on one kind of theory at a time is that the teaching task can then be seen as a matter of devising programmes for the development of specific skills and we may then try to cover these exhaustively by providing a wide range of carefully structured teaching materials. It is important to remind ourselves, therefore, that only a very small proportion of the words a child learns to read are acquired by direct instruction; in addition, the vast majority of phonic 'rules', morpho-phonemic regularities, or grammatical relationships that actually influence a child's reading have never been expressly taught. Furthermore, many of those children who excel in reading, and in language generally, have acquired their high levels of competence without being exposed to anything remotely resembling either the highly-structured and educationally-emaciated reading or study skills laboratory, or the manipulations of those who are concerned more with the formal processes of language and reading than with the educationally purposeful pursuit of information, inspiration or ideas. By working from specific theory to specific practice, we usually end up by imposing a wide range of learning activities which are largely unnecessary and which detract from those more fundamental educational processes which tend, by and large, to make them so.

Perhaps the answer is that we should not be talking about reading in the first place – at least not as a separate study. It is not reading per se that concerns us but learning. Reading is only one part of the total process of learning in the classroom. We may well have done much more harm than good by separating it out from the general context of learning in the first place.

By way of aside, it is interesting to recall that 'membership in professional associations of educators or subject matter teachers was a favourable indicator [of reading achievement]' in the international survey reported earlier. Presumably teachers who join such associations do so because they are concerned with the general problem of how their pupils learn – and about ways of helping them. Indeed, to many teachers it will be no surprise to learn that a teacher's concern about learning in general tends to be associated with higher reading achievement on the part of his or her pupils!

If, then, the primary focus in teacher training, initial or inservice, is to be on the general question of how we can most effectively facilitate learning, not reading or language, we need to start, I would suggest, by getting student teachers and practising teachers to look first at what learning is already going on in the classroom. We need to get them to look at what their pupils actually do during a given period, what they are actually learning, and what the benefits are of what they have done and learned. In addition, however, they need to look at pupils over a prolonged period and ask themselves what it all adds up to for any individual pupil. The general approach referred to here is exemplified in Open University Course P234, *Curriculum in Action*. This course is currently being adapted so that the materials will lend themselves more readily to use by groups of teachers working in school-centred curriculum development activities. The general approach was also a central feature in the DES funded Initial

Teaching-Inservice Education Project reported by Ashton et al. (1983).

The crunch comes, of course, in asking this question, 'What does it all add up to?' Just imagine what we should find if we were to make substantial longitudinal studies of the curriculum as experienced by individual children over the whole of their school lives? What do they actually spend most of their time doing? How much do they actually learn of what we teach – and what other kinds of learning take place that we did not specifically intend? At the end of the day, how much of this has contributed significantly to their development as human beings? How much has been neutral? How much has actually been adverse in its effects?

If we take these broader educational questions as our starting point we can then justifiably go on to ask some more specific questions, focusing first, perhaps, on language. What proportion of each child's time is spent in:

1 sitting passively, either listening or not listening, while the teacher talks;
2 talking to other children, the teacher, other adults;
3 talking about priorities, as a prelude to decision-making, strategies, as a prelude to action, the task in hand, as an aspect of co-operative endeavour, or outcomes and manner of achievement, as a means of learning from experience?

If education is to provide a sound foundation for individual development, allied to social and environmental responsibility, then operational questions such as the above, rather than limited-focus theoretical questions, must provide the starting point, both in establishing priorities and in seeking valid evidence for assessing our current effectiveness. Only through pursuing such questions, and their practical implications, can we begin to identify which of the possible contributions deriving from such disciplines as philosophy, sociology, psychology or linguistics might actually assist professional judgement.

Naturally, the same holds for reading. In the case of children who are getting beyond the early stages of learning to read, we might ask such questions as:

1 What proportion of each child's time is spent in reading tasks set by the teacher, and answering questions set by teacher or textbook/work-card author, rather than by the child him or herself?
2 Within the general pattern of negotiation outlined above, what proportion of each child's time is spent in:
   (a) deciding what additional information is needed, and why;
   (b) identifying possible sources, pre-viewing and selecting sources, planning appropriate ways of recording information (e.g. tables, diagrams, storage/retrieval formats, etc.);
   (c) skimming, scanning, searching, selecting, evaluating and organising information according to a well-defined purpose, following the strategy previously determined by the reader him or herself;
   (d) evaluating the reading outcome/s and taking any further action that may be necessary in the light of further discussion or personal review?

The questions provide a broad indication of what is involved in effective reading on the part of autonomous, responsible adults. And, like the related questions on language generally, they provide an appropriate starting point both for a review of theory and an orderly appraisal of relevance and priorities.

By way of example, current work on schema theory might be reviewed by any tutor who wants to involve teachers in a study of comprehension. One aspect of this study might be an examination of the effectiveness of different kinds of pre-task intervention. The teacher, however, taking a broader view of the kind indicated above, should in this context adopt the position of the apocryphal Irishman who was asked the way by a passing motorist: 'If I was you, I wouldn't be starting from here in the first place!' For the teacher, in deciding how best to develop competent reading, needs to start with the normal everyday life situation where it is the reader who decides whether to read, what to read, and how to organise the outcomes so that they can be achieved. Thus, a contents x type-of-risk matrix might be the best way of comparing the cover provided by different insurance policies whereas constructing a very simple flow diagram, or even a list, may be the best way of learning what to do in the event of making a claim.

If the normal reading task is not determined by someone else's selection of text, purpose, and schematic pre-task intervention, but by the reader's own purpose and outcome requirements, then if this makes some kinds of reading more difficult – that's life. We simply have to get on with it, not abandon the more difficult tasks. They all have to be included in the curriculum and, when included, must not be submerged by a plethora of other reading activities that are counter-productive.

By starting at the academic research end of the spectrum, the teacher can develop hopelessly inappropriate priorities and practices. Research by the classroom teacher then typically follows along the same narrow lines and legitimises inferior educational practice by investing it with a halo of spurious academic respectability.

A singular advantage of a more realistic approach in the design of courses is that not only teachers (and/or student teachers) but tutors also can always begin by observing current practice afresh. They can then compare and contrast this using criteria which they jointly identify as being consistent with their own educational philosophy, the realities of the particular school and the present and future demands of everyday life. Together they can review the practical possibilities for developing a richer and more realistic array of educational experiences, noting particularly the demands this would make on the language and reading abilities of pupils, and how much reading and language development takes place automatically as they modify the curriculum. The tutor can then help the students/teachers to identify the relevant literature and to approach their own studies in the manner indicated by the questions set out above for developing effective reading in their own pupils. Thus tutors and teachers can practise what they preach!

If both tutors and teachers can be encouraged to adopt this sort of approach to what is actually happening in their classrooms and to accept increasing responsibility for working out their own solutions, we may begin to see some much more profitable approaches to the development of effective reading. This may not at first please the producers of existing reading schemes and workshops, but it opens up possibilities for their development of a much more stimulating range of resource materials. It will no doubt cause much heart-searching among those with a vested academic interest in courses specialising narrowly on reading or language – but it eliminates the embarrassment of persisting with manifestly inappropriate courses and allows tutors to escape from the narrow constraints of the ivory tower. It may even help teachers to inject a much needed dose of realism into reading education.

References

Ashton, P.M.E., Henderson, E.S., Merritt, J.E. and Mortimer, D.J. (1983) *Teacher Education in the Classroom*. Croom Helm.

Corder, R. (1971) *The Information Base for Reading*, National Centre for Educational Research and Development, Project No. 0-9031. Educational Testing Service, Berkeley, California.

DES (1975) *A Language for Life* (The Bullock report). HMSO.

Durkin, D. (1974) 'A six year study of children who learned to read in school at the age of four', *Reading Research Quarterly, 10*, 9-61.

Hewison, J. (1982) 'Parental involvement in the teaching of reading', *Remedial Education, 17*, 156-62.

Thorndike, R.L. (1973) *Reading Comprehension Education in Fifteen Countries: International Studies in Evaluation, III*. International Association for the Evaluation of Educational Achievement (IEA), Wiley.

Tizard, J., Schofield, W.N. and Hewison, J. (1982) 'Collaboration between teachers and parents in assisting children's reading', *British Journal of Educational Psychology, 52*, 1-15.

Contributors

Asher Cashdan is Head of the Department of Communication Studies and Dean of the Faculty of Cultural Studies at Sheffield City Polytechnic.

Gordon Wells is Professor of Education at the Ontario Institute for Studies in Education. He was formerly Reader in Education at the University of Bristol.

Geoffrey Underwood is a Lecturer in Psychology at the University of Nottingham.

Jean Underwood is a Senior Lecturer in Educational Computing at Derbyshire College of Higher Education.

Colin Harrison is a Lecturer in Education at the University of Nottingham.

John Harris is a Principal Lecturer in English and Co-ordinator of the Language Development Centre at Sheffield City Polytechnic.

Helen Arnold is a Lecturer and Consultant in Reading and Language. She was formerly English Adviser to Suffolk Local Education Authority and a Researcher on the Schools Council *Extending Beginning Reading* Project at the University of Manchester.

David Wray is a Lecturer in Education at University College, Cardiff.

David Williams is a teacher in the Special Needs Department of Benfield School, Newcastle-upon-Tyne.

Peter Brinton is Deputy Head of St Columb Minor Primary School, Newquay, Cornwall.

John Merritt is Professor of Teacher Education at the Open University.

Index